Christm...
Darli...
Love P...
Many more happy days
at Lords.

PAVILIONS *of*
SPLENDOUR

PAVILIONS *of* SPLENDOUR

An Architectural History of Lord's

Edited by

DUFF HART-DAVIS

Foreword by

HRH THE DUKE OF EDINBURGH

methuen

Published by Methuen 2004

1 3 5 7 9 10 8 6 4 2

First published in Great Britain 2004
by Methuen Publishing Limited
215 Vauxhall Bridge Road
London SW1V 1EJ

www.methuen.co.uk

Methuen Publishing Limited Reg. No. 3543167

A CIP catalogue record for this book is available from the British Library

ISBN 0 413 77458 9

Printed and bound in Great Britain by the Bath Press

Contents

This book is dedicated to the memory of
Michael Wolton, Assistant to the Curator,
who died tragically on 19 March 2004.

Acknowledgements

The original idea that this book should be written came from David Cheshire, a member of MCC, in 2001.

The editor and contributors would like to thank the following for their help and advice:

Michael Baker, Rebecca Chipchase, Sir Anthony Denny, Maurice de Rohan, Hubert Doggart, Martin Ellis, Eleanor Gawne and her staff in the Library of the Royal Institute of British Architects, Sir Roger Gibbs, David Glover, Sir Nicholas Grimshaw, David Harriss, Stuart Hibberdine, Sir Michael Hopkins, Dr Gerald Howat, Jan Kaplicky, Rob Kinch, Amanda Levete, Alex Lifschutz, the staff of the London Metropolitan Archive, Russell Long of the Louis de Soissons Partnership, Guy Macaulay, David Morley, Andrew Mytom, Sue Offen, Panos Panayiotou, Radhika Ponniah, John Pringle, John Qualtrough, Andrew Rees, Dr Jane Ridley, Irving Rosenwater, Dennis Silk, Dr Gavin Stamp, Nicholas Thompson, John Thornton, Peter Tummons, William Taylor.

Much help was also given by the personnel at Lord's, principally Stephen Green (Curator until September 2003), David Batts (Deputy Chief Executive), Adam Chadwick (Curator), Colin Maynard (Assistant Secretary – Membership), Stephen Parris (Estates Manager), Glenys Williams (Archivist and Historian), Ken Daldry and the late Michael Wolton.

Unless otherwise specified, all quotations are taken from MCC minutes.

MCC is grateful to Fleming Family & Partners for their generous contribution towards the cost of the illustrations.

Foreword

by HRH The Duke of Edinburgh

Lord's is best known as the home of Marylebone Cricket Club, and as the headquarters of the game of cricket. Neither the ground nor the Club would have attained that status had the members not built the stands to attract spectators and the facilities to attract members. This history of the far-sighted developments, and the courageous financial investments which made them possible, complements the story of the development of the game in this country and across the globe. It may come as a bit of a surprise to find that the members of a once almost rural cricket club in north London should have had the enterprise and foresight to lead their club to become the world governing body of cricket for over a hundred years.

PAVILIONS *of* SPLENDOUR

1

The Beginning

1787–1837

In 1787 the President of the famous Hambledon Cricket Club in Hampshire was George Finch, the ninth Earl of Winchilsea. His Mecca in London was the White Conduit Club in Islington, then still a rural area on the outskirts of the city. It was there that he met an interesting young man from Thirsk, in Yorkshire, called Thomas Lord.

Lord served the White Conduit Club as a ground bowler and general factotum, and in the course of his work he was introduced to many of the notables of the day, including Winchilsea and Charles Lennox, later the fourth Duke of Richmond. Winchilsea was particularly keen that Lord should establish facilities for a cricket club in a more central part of London: he told him that he could call the ground after his own name, and that he would be indemnified against any financial loss he might incur in undertaking such an ambitious project.

Thus encouraged, Lord obtained a lease on part of the Portman family estate in the area then known as Dorset Fields (a small portion of which survives today in Dorset Square, approximately half-way between Baker Street and Marylebone stations). Here was founded the Marylebone Cricket Club. 31 May 1787 was the momentous day on which the first match took place on the new

Portrait of Thomas Lord.

GRAND CRICKET MATCH, *played in Lord's Ground Mary-le-bone, on June 20 & following day between the EARLS of WINCHELSEA & DARNLEY for 1000 Guineas.*

Published July 1st 1793. by I. Whible Warwick Square London

colours by Henry Matthews, depicting the presentation of colours to the Second and Third Regiments of the Royal East India Volunteers in 1797.

A better impression of the ground can be gained from Thomas Stothard's painting in the Bank of England Museum, which shows Lord standing on a rostrum to watch the wives of the Bank's directors present colours to members of the Bank of England Volunteers. The picture was commissioned in 1799, and the area round about still looks very rural.

Both the *Sporting Magazine* print and the Bank of England painting depict a small pavilion. The British Library watercolours unfortunately do not show any buildings on the ground – but a little more detail about the first Lord's is happily provided by an unlikely source.

In 1810 one Dr Nathaniel Highmore wrote a book called *Ius Ecclesiasticum Anglicanum*, subtitled 'The Government of the Church of England Exemplified and Illustrated'. The author was an embittered cleric who had been prevented by the Archbishop of Canterbury from acting as a stipendiary clergyman while appearing at the same time as an advocate in the ecclesiastical court. Highmore was annoyed that the Reverend Lord Frederick Beauclerk was free (probably because he was the son of a duke) to spend hours on end playing cricket, despite the fact that he held the living of St Albans.

On 23 June 1808 Highmore discovered that Beauclerk was to play at Lord's, and wrote:

> I went on the day advertised, viz. Thursday the 23rd of June, to Lord's cricket-ground, to see the athletic performances of the Reverend and beneficed cricket-player and gambler. Having paid my sixpence, I was admitted. After walking some little time

ground. Middlesex (with two of Derbyshire and one of Kent) played Essex (with two given men) for 100 guineas, and won by ninety-three runs.

We know tantalisingly little about that first ground. An illustration in the *Sporting Magazine* for 1 July 1793 shows the 'Grand Cricket Match, played in Lord's Ground, Mary-le-bone, on June 20 & following day between the Earls of Winchelsea & Darnley for 1000 Guineas' – but this is the only surviving picture of cricket in Dorset Fields. Fortunately, other illustrations show more of the original Lord's, which proved a useful place on which to hold parades as the fear of a Napoleonic invasion caused a great upsurge of patriotism. The British Library owns two fine water-about the spacious area destined for this very curious clerical exhibition, I went up to the booth.

When I stood there, on the outside (for entrance seemed to belong only to the initiated and privileged) for a short time, I noticed a man, coming out of the booth, dressed in a white hat, a coloured handkerchief round his neck, striped trousers, and a square kind of coat, such as I have seen stage coachmen, horse-dealers, and keepers of livery stables dressed in, and which I have since been informed is called a groom's coat.

The wearer of this flamboyant outfit of course turned out to be Lord Frederick – but sadly for the architectural historian, Highmore was more interested in laying the aristocrat's alleged misdemeanours before the Primate of All England than in describing the buildings of the original Lord's.

As London expanded, the rent for the ground increased sharply; but on 15 October 1808 Lord was astute enough to hire the Brick Field and the Great Field at North Bank, on the Eyre Estate in rural St John's Wood, for a term of eighty years, free of land-tax and tithe, at £54 per annum. In order that 'the noblemen and gentlemen of the MCC should be able to play on the same footing as before,' he had the turf transferred from Dorset Fields – no mean task, without machines. The ground was ready for use by 1809, but the second Lord's did not open officially until 8 May 1811.

No one seems to have much liked the new ground, and not many matches were played on it. Salvation came from an unlikely source when Parliament resolved that the Regent's Canal should be cut right through the playing area. There was thus no need to argue about the desirability or otherwise of moving to pastures new. Once more the Eyre family came to Lord's aid, providing another plot slightly further to the north on a new eighty-year lease commencing in 1813. Yet again the turf was transferred, in time for the start of the 1814 season.

Lord's third ground was said to have been built on rubble excavated when the Maida Hill tunnel was constructed for the canal. It opened literally with a bang. Four days before the advertised opening date there was an explosion at the 'new Lord's cricket ground public house, Marylebone Fields'. It is not clear why the landlady had gunpowder in her possession – but she was seriously burned.

The first official function was probably a quieter affair. After consecrating the adjacent St John's Wood Chapel (now the local parish church), the Bishop of London was given a reception on the ground, and the *Morning Post* for 7 May 1814 carried this announcement:

> T. Lord respectfully informs the Noblemen, Gentlemen, Members of the Marylebone and St John's Wood Cricket Clubs, that the new ground is completely ready for playing on and that the first meeting of the Marylebone Club will be on Monday 9th May and continue every Monday, Wednesday and Friday during the season. The New Road leading to it is commodiously finished, the entrance to which is opposite Marylebone Workhouse or up Baker Street North, which is upwards of half a mile nearer than up the old road up Lisson Grove.

The first match took place on 22 June 1814, when MCC beat Hertfordshire by an innings and twenty-seven runs. For a few years all seemed to be serene; but in 1825 Lord shocked the cricketing world by announcing that the Eyre Estate had given him permission to build houses on part of the outfield. Only a very small area would be left.

No one was more alarmed than William Ward, MP for the City of London and a director of the Bank of England (it was he who in 1820 had made the record score for Lord's of 278 when batting for MCC against Norfolk). He wrote a cheque for £5,000 to buy the lease from Lord, and thus saved the ground for cricket.

His immediate reward was a baptism of fire. On Friday, 29 July 1825, the pavilion burned to ashes, as *The Times* reported next day:

> From the nature of the materials, which were chiefly of wood, albeit lately enlarged and beautified at great expense, the fire in a very short time defied the power of the fire-engines and water, if there had been a sufficient supply, which happened not to be the case. In about an hour and a half after the commencement of the fire, the whole pavilion was reduced to a heap of ruins, saving only the foundation.

The *Morning Post* for 30 July mischievously added: 'It is a curious fact that a grand match was to have been played yesterday in the ground, between the scholars of Harrow School and Eton College, and that some of the parties enjoyed themselves in the early part of Thursday.' On Sunday, 31 July, *John Bull* told a more doleful story: 'There was in the pavilion a large and valuable stock of wine, the property of the subscribers, which, along with all their cricketing apparatus, no longer exists'.

In spite of the disaster, the match advertised for the very next day took place – but all the club's early records had gone up in smoke.

After the fire the MCC lost no time in building a new pavilion, which was ready in time for the anniversary dinner on 11 May 1826. It was a utilitarian building, with a low elevation, but in 1865 it was enlarged by the addition of two wings, a basement and a new frontage.

Thomas Stothard's painting showing the presentation of colours to the Bank of England Volunteers on Thomas Lord's first ground in 1799.

In 1835 William Ward transferred the lease of Lord's, with fifty-eight years left, to the businessman and entrepreneur, J. H. Dark, for £2,000 and an annuity of £425. The print made to celebrate the Jubilee Match held two years later on the Club's fiftieth anniversary shows a number of buildings around the perimeter of the ground, of which the only one surviving today is the Roman Catholic Church in Lisson Grove.

The best account of the ground in this period was given by Sir Spencer Ponsonby-Fane, the *éminence grise* of Lord's for many years, and Treasurer for a record period from 1878 to 1915. He wrote in 1914 about his memories of the ground eighty years previously:

> Whilst I was still a lad, Mr Dark, then proprietor of the ground and who paid all expenses connected with it, presented me with a bat and the 'Freedom of the Ground', as he called it. From that time I was there continually, and I may almost say I have lived there up to the present day.

Recording all the changes that had taken place over the years, Sir Spencer contrasted the 'rough and simple habits' of earlier times with the 'luxury of the present day.' Earlier, he wrote, the pavilion was a small, one-roomed building surrounded with a few laurels and shrubs, and capable of holding forty or fifty members. In it sat Lord Frederick Beauclerk, 'then the autocrat of the club and of cricket in general, laying down the law and organising the game'.

> Then there was the public house, a long low building on the south side, separated from the ground by a row of clipped lime trees and a few green benches on which the thirsty spectators smoked long pipes and enjoyed drinks. Round the ground were more of these small benches without backs, and a pot-boy walked round with a supply of beer, a porter for the public who had no other means of refreshing themselves. Excepting these benches there were no seats for spectators.
>
> At the south-east corner of the ground there were large stacks of willow blocks to be seasoned and made into bats in the workshop adjoining. On the upper north-east corner was a large sheep pen. In the centre of the ground opposite the Pavilion was a square patch of grass which was kept constantly rolled and taken care of. No scythe was allowed to touch it and mowing machines were not then invented.
>
> The rest of the ground was ridge and furrow – not very easy for playing on, nor made any easier by the number of old pitches which abounded, for on non-match days the public could have a pitch for a shilling, a sum which included the use of stumps, bat and ball, the last-named selected from half a dozen or so from the capacious breeches of 'Steevie' Slatter, Mr Dark's factotum, which never seemed to be empty.
>
> The grass as I have said was never mowed. It was usually kept down by a flock of sheep which was penned up on match days and on Saturdays four or five hundred were on the ground on their way to the Monday Smithfield Market. It was wonderful to see how they cleared the herbage.

In 1889 the second pavilion was taken down and rebuilt on the Ranfold Estate at Slinfold in Sussex. Here it survived until the early 1980s, when it was demolished to make way – alas – for a property development. Latterly it seems to have been used as a glorified gardening shed. It is best illustrated in the 1874 painting by Henry Barraud, in the Museum of London. There is also a drawing by André Bourdillon, with additions by Gustav Doré, in the Glynn Vivian Art Gallery in Swansea.

The Grand Jubilee match played at Lord's on 10 July 1837 between the North and South of England to commemorate the fiftieth anniversary of the Club.

J. H. Dark, proprietor of Lord's until 1864.

2

The Victorian Era

1837–1901

In 1837, while Great Britain rejoiced in the accession of the young Queen Victoria, MCC too had cause for celebration. The Club was observing its Golden Jubilee, and this fiftieth anniversary was commemorated with a Grand Cricket Match, which took place on 10 and 11 July between sides representing North and South. It was a splendid affair, although the match itself received little publicity, taking place as it did just two days after the funeral of William IV.

During the next sixty-four years of Victoria's reign, cricket became respectable, and MCC was transformed from an exclusive club for energetic gentry into an institution worthy of a great empire. The game was no longer the domain of gambling rakes or dissipated earls who viewed matches only as occasions for wagers. Cricket was swept along on a tide of reform and muscular Christianity, emanating from the public schools, which were transforming a series of riotous folk pastimes into rule-bound, manly pursuits intended to forge the characters of budding empire-builders.

These changes were accompanied by the growth of cricket as a spectator sport, and it was also during the late Victorian era that the game came of age; the County Championship was formalised and the first international fixtures played. Wherever Victoria's empire-builders went, cricket soon followed, and by the turn of the century the game was truly international. By 1903–04, when the MCC sent its first official tour overseas, the Club had become the undisputed authority on the game. It was the arbiter on all matters concerning the laws, and the leader in promoting the health and spirit of the game that symbolised, above all others, notions of British leadership and fair play throughout the Empire.

As cricket became a pastime pursued by the expanding bourgeoisie, membership of the MCC grew likewise: between 1845 and 1900 it rose from just 465 to 5,000. The increased numbers meant that more extensive facilities were required, and it was during this period that the Club embarked upon what was to be, until the late twentieth century, its greatest building spree, developing virtually all the land surrounding the playing area with a variety of stands and other facilities for members. This process culminated in 1890–91 with Thomas Verity's fine, high Victorian pavilion, the only building from that era which remains standing today.

Expansion of the MCC, however, was not inevitable, and certainly not without its share of crises. Indeed, for the first quarter of a century after its golden jubilee there was a real possibility that Lord's, if not MCC itself, would fail to survive. London was expanding rapidly, building land was at a premium, and MCC held no share in the actual ownership of Lord's. The Club's struggle to obtain the ground for itself in the end proved the turning point in MCC's fortunes.

In 1835 the leasehold of Lord's had been transferred from William Ward to J.H. Dark. Dark was the son of a saddler, born in the Edgware Road, and began his association with Lord's at the age of ten when he earned pocket money as a fielder at MCC's first ground in Dorset Square.

The ground that Dark inherited was very much a rural one, on the outskirts of London, and like a village green in appearance, with post-and-chain fencing surrounding an uneven playing area which was, for many years, regarded as one of the most dangerous

in the land. Its ridge-and-furrow surface was kept mown by sheep, and pitch-markings were cut with a knife – a surface not at all favoured by batsmen having to contend with the new, faster, round-arm bowling technique that had been legalised in 1835. Sir Pelham Warner, in his book *Lord's 1787–1945*, gives a vivid description of the ground as it was in 1841. Lord's had:

Lord's in 1837, showing the sheep used to keep the grass down.

ENCAMPMENT OF IOWAY INDIANS, LORD'S CRICKET-GROUND.—THE WELCOME SPEECH.

THE IOWAY INDIANS.

The Ioway Indians
at Lord's in 1844.

for a number of unusual displays, including an encampment of the Ioway Indians, with displays of dancing and archery. He was, however, a loyal supporter of MCC, and ploughed much of his profit back into facilities that, he hoped, would encourage the expansion of the Club.

In 1837 the only buildings of any significance were a pavilion and a tavern. By 1838 the pavilion had been lit by gas, and a new assembly room had been built over the parlour of the tavern. A room at the east end of the tavern was converted into a billiards room, a bowling green was laid down on the west side, and Dark had obtained extra land at the nursery end which he intended as an area for archery practice.

In 1838 he invested in the construction of a real tennis court, on the east side of the ground, where the Mound Stand is now situated. The MCC's President, Benjamin Aislabie, laid the first stone of the court on 15 October, and the building was completed, at a cost of £4,000, the following spring. Facilities offered to members included dressing rooms with hot and cold baths, couches for rest after a game and two of the finest billiard tables

a cottage-like pavilion with a few shrubs in front of it. Sandwiches and beer were the only refreshments except for an ordinary [set meal] at a tavern which the gentlemen never went to. There was a miniature hill and valley between the farthest corner of the pavilion and the lower wicket, and Lord's was more like a field pure and simple; but the rigour of the game was insisted on, and it was a ground to test a man's batting ability.

Dark did not find it easy to make money from cricket. Between 1830 and 1863 there were never more than twenty-three MCC matches played at Lord's in a year – sometimes as few as nine. Dark supplemented his income by using Lord's as a show ground

The first tennis court, completed in 1839, standing on the site of the Mound Stand.

for the gentlemen's amusement. As hoped, this innovation proved a popular inducement to new members, 150 of whom enrolled in the months following the completion of the court.

Over the next twenty-five years a number of other smaller improvements were made. In 1839 a 'scoring perch' was erected: this consisted of an elevated platform, some eight feet high, on top of which sat the match scorer. This vantage-point, reached by a ladder, afforded the official an excellent view of the play, and also removed him from the continued attentions of the cricket-watching public, thus allowing for more accurately recorded games.

In 1842 Dark made a running track around the ground which measured 640 feet long by 7 feet 6 inches wide. Some sixty loads of gravel were used in its construction, and it was well patronised by MCC members. Dark also used it to promote events such as pony-racing and stone-picking contests, which were popular with the general public. A racquets court was added to the tennis court building in 1844, and in 1847 a small room was built on the north side of the pavilion for use by the professional cricketers who, until then, had had to enter the playing area through the public entrance. On 26 June 1848 a portable printing tent was introduced by Frederick Lillywhite, and the public could, for the first time, obtain scorecards. The structure was removed after each great match.

In 1849 the ground was properly drained for the first time, at Dark's expense, for £300. Fifty drains, measuring a total length of just over five miles, were laid two-and-a-half feet under the surface and covered with a mixture of rubble and oyster shells. This helped to improve wickets, but the ground remained notoriously uneven. Dark also planted 400 trees around the perimeter, a legacy which, to this day, helps Lord's retain its village atmosphere.

Dark did his best to draw attractions to the ground, and MCC struggled to maintain its match schedule on an extremely tight budget. Membership had increased, but the irregularities in the pitch continued to make the venue an unpopular one with players, many of whom preferred to play across the river at the Oval. There is no doubt that the MCC was in decline and facing a crisis.

Lord Harris, who was born in 1851, recalled the ground as it was when he was a boy in his 1914 book *Lord's and the MCC*:

> Dark's house was in the left-hand corner of the ground going in, and the only other buildings were a pavilion – a green-painted wooden building with a kind of dressing room at the back – tennis court and a rustic tavern with bow windows and a row of very leafy trees in front. On one side of the pavilion stood a row of pollard trees, and behind them were the beautiful gardens, four acres in extent, belonging to Landseer, the great animal painter.

Despite these fond memories, as Tony Lewis wrote in *Double Century* in 1987, 'in truth Lord's was an atrocious playing surface and not a comfortable place even for members to watch . . . Dark's ground was tatty and deteriorating'. Criticisms were made about the lack of accommodation for ladies, and of proper dining facilities. A number of members suggested that a new ground be built at Brompton, and even MCC's authority over the laws of the game was called into question. To make matters worse, when, in 1860, the Eyre Estate sold the freehold of Lord's at public auction, MCC did not even bother to bid. The ground was bought by a Mr Isaac Moses for £7,000 – and the MCC would in the future pay dearly for this lack of foresight.

In 1864 Dark, now almost 70, decided to relinquish his interest in the ground. He had been approached by Moses, who wished to purchase the leasehold. This, along with the freehold he already owned, would enable him to build houses on the site. Dark, fortunately for MCC, remained loyal, and offered the Club first refusal on his property for the sum of £15,000. His actions in this matter almost certainly saved Lord's from the developer, and forced MCC into making a firm decision about its future. As Tony Lewis described it in *Double Century*:

> The Marylebone Club was facing the most serious choice of its life . . . to go out to find the real public it claimed to serve, or to sit in a crumbling pavilion, smoking cigars, babbling on about the cricket of a bygone age.

MCC signalled its intentions with the appointment of R. A. Fitzgerald, a man of great energy and vision, as Honorary Secretary. He began immediately to turn the fortunes of the Club round by negotiating the purchase of Dark's interest in Lord's. At a general meeting of MCC on 8 April 1864, he urged the Club to 'take steps to secure that place which had always been considered the head-quarters of cricket.' The minutes record that he went on to argue:

> Cricket was the only exclusively English game which they had, and no other game could be compared to it for its manly and invigorating nature . . . The Marylebone Club should hold a position in the cricket world similar to that which was maintained by the Jockey Club in the racing community, and as a first step to that they should secure to themselves permanent headquarters at Lord's Cricket Ground, where laws could be

R. A. Fitzgerald, Secretary 1863–76, by Alfred Bryan.

regularly made and carried out, and where all questions relating to the game might be settled for the interest and undeniable advantage to all cricketing classes in the United Kingdom.

The land upon which Lord's stood, he added, was a very desirable building spot and, if MCC did not take this opportunity, it would find itself without a ground and with very little prospect of finding another within reasonable distance of London. The meeting agreed unanimously to buy Dark's interest in the ground for £11,000, plus £1,500 for fixtures and furniture. They also authorised Fitzgerald to negotiate with Moses a new 99-year lease at an annual rent of £550. It was proposed that these costs be met by a voluntary donation fund, to which the Prince of Wales gave 100 guineas, and by creating a number of life memberships at £30 each. Dark, accommodating as always, eased the Club's financial burden by agreeing to accept payment in instalments at five per cent interest on the amount owing.

MCC had thus secured, at the very least, its immediate future in St John's Wood, and to celebrate Fitzgerald sprang into action with a number of projects that would improve facilities for members and public alike. In the winter of 1864 a large portion of the ground was levelled and re-turfed. The racquets court was fully restored, and plans were put under way for improvements to the pavilion, which continued over the next two years.

A new wing was added to each end of the structure, a room made in the basement for the players, and alterations carried out to include a library, committee room and dressing rooms, as well as several minor apartments that served as members' accommodation. The roof of the building, constructed on Bunnings' patent principle, was altered to provide a large number of extra seats, access to which was achieved by the installation of two wide staircases. This work was carried out by building contractors Temple & Foster at a cost of £1,000.

The advantages enjoyed by MCC in owning the leasehold of Lord's prompted Fitzgerald to suggest that the Club might approach Moses with a view to securing the freehold. The Club paid dearly for its failure to bid for it in 1860, but eventually a bargain was struck at £18,313 6s 6d – nearly three times the

amount paid by Moses (who by this time had changed his name to Marsden).

MCC was once again fortunate in its benefactors, and on this occasion the money for the purchase was raised thanks to an influential member, William Nicholson, proprietor of Nicholson's gin, who offered to advance the sum on a mortgage on the premises. At a special general meeting held on 2 May 1866 his

The second pavilion, built for the 1826 season after the fire of the previous year. Shown here in 1874 with MCC members. *(Museum of London)*

proposal was unanimously accepted, and MCC could now call Lord's its own. (Some people believe – although there is no documentary evidence to confirm it – that MCC adopted its colours, which first appeared in the 1860s, as a mark of gratitude to Nicholson, whose gin label was red and yellow. Of course such sponsorship, if it existed, could not be spoken of at the time.)

In order to pay off its loan, MCC needed to recruit more members, and to do that the Club had to transform Lord's into a venue fit for cricket's foremost club. Increased attendance required extended accommodation but, after the purchase of the freehold, MCC's finances were limited. Fitzgerald therefore proposed the formation of a private syndicate of MCC members who would finance the building of a new stand. MCC was given the right to purchase the stand at any time in the future, but, in the meantime, all profits would go to the investors.

This new building, the first Grand Stand at Lord's, ran along the west side of the ground. It was 175 feet long and 30 feet high, with seating on five levels. A permanent printing office was installed at the back of the building; members of the Press were, for the first time, given their own accommodation, and there were a number of refreshment bars and toilet facilities. In addition, a private box was added to the top of the structure for the exclusive use of the Prince of Wales. The Grand Stand was built in the winter of 1866–67 and was used for the first time on 27 May 1867. Two years later MCC took up its option to purchase the stand, which it did on 1 September 1869 for the sum of £1,703 7s 8d.

In October 1867 the Committee agreed to pull down the existing tavern, which no longer met the Club's requirements. Once more MCC gratefully accepted a £4,000 advance from Mr Nicholson to pay for a new hotel and tavern building. Paraire & Co. were appointed architects, and a tender for the construction work, amounting to £3,983 3s 0d, was accepted from Ager's, a firm of builders.

One of the men then employed on the ground was William Slatter, and in his memoir *Recollections of Lord's and the MCC*, written in 1914, he recorded numerous problems that occurred with the foundations of the hotel, which were, in his opinion, dug too deep and were prone to flooding. He reported that the centre of the building sank two inches in the few years after construction and, as a result, had to be altered and strengthened on several occasions. On the whole, however, MCC were delighted with their new building, which afforded a double entrance on to the ground, as well as providing extra seats for spectators. Mr Day, landlord of the old tavern, continued as tenant at a rent of £400 per annum. Fitzgerald's efforts on behalf of MCC were rewarded with an annual salary of £400, and he became the Club's first permanent secretary.

In 1869 MCC purchased Guy's Nursery, a narrow strip of land on the east side of the ground. This allowed free entry for all carriages, whereas previously the Club had had to pay £20 per annum to bring them in. The Annual General Meeting in 1869 also reported that the tennis and racquets courts had been fully restored and improvements made. This building was further enhanced in 1872 when a large clock, presented by Lord Ebury, was placed in the sidelights facing the playing area.

Wisden Cricketers' Almanack of 1870 gives an account of an Eton and Harrow match which provides an idea of how Lord's appeared at this time,

The Grand Stand was thronged . . . [and] the Pavilion seats and roof were crowded with members and their friends. 'The Ring' was deeper and more densely packed, and the outer ring of

The hotel and tavern built in 1867,
providing a double entrance to the ground.

carriages more extensive, than at any previous match. Such an assemblage of rank, fashion and numbers has never before been seen at Lord's. It was computed that quite 30,000 visitors attended the ground on those two memorable days . . . Down by Mr Dark's house, up by the north-east corner, and fronting the whole row of well-known dwarf chestnut trees, the accidental but graceful grouping of ladies elegantly attired added a picturesque brilliancy to the old ground not seen at other matches.

Lord's had arrived. It had become very much part of the English social scene – a place where the great and the good came to see and to be seen.

MCC's programme of improvement and repair continued throughout the 1870s and 1880s. By the spring of 1874 the great work of raising and re-levelling the whole of the playing area was complete, and the benefits were immediately apparent. The ground soon lost its reputation of having a most dangerous pitch, and MCC was at last able to offer one of England's finest playing areas, alongside its unmatched facilities. The hotel was being constantly renewed and extra facilities, including a billiards room for the exclusive use of MCC members, were built above the tennis court. Three rows of fixed seats were also placed, for public use, on an embankment at the north-west corner of the ground. By 1875 improvements and repairs were now so frequently required that an architect and surveyor were engaged at a fixed salary. William Slatter was placed in charge of the painting and decoration department and was later promoted to Clerk of Works.

In 1875 ill-health forced the retirement of the Secretary, Fitzgerald. He was replaced by Henry Perkins who, determined to carry on the good work, added, in 1876, further dressing rooms, extra seating to the pavilion and extended the professionals' area.

In 1881 luncheon rooms were built to the west side of the hotel yard on the site of the Armoury. The building had a flat roof to allow for seating, although, as Slatter recalls, no stairway was included in the original plans, so that an outside staircase had to be added. Included in the facilities were a refreshment bar, an extra kitchen, a service room, a storeroom and a cold-storage room that was fitted with freezing machines. Once more there were drainage problems, and Slatter describes how, one Christmas night, a water main burst in St John's Wood Road, flooding the basement to a depth of nine inches. The luncheon rooms were, however, extremely popular with members, who previously had dined in the pavilion. Refreshments could now be served at all times, not just during breaks in play.

In 1885 an additional wing was added to the Grand Stand, and a terrace erected around the A Enclosure (which filled the space between the pavilion and the Grand Stand). A new set of bathrooms was added to the pavilion, with hot and cold running water, and the interior of the tavern was rebuilt. A tarmac footpath was laid from the entrance to the pavilion. This was continued around the ground towards the tennis court in 1886. Also at this time MCC began a policy of purchasing the leasehold of properties surrounding the ground in Elm Tree Road, Grove End Road and St John's Wood Road. This was intended to provide the Club with a valuable source of income.

In 1887 MCC celebrated its centenary, and at the AGM that year the Committee were pleased to congratulate the members on the flourishing condition of the Club. Membership was increasing apace, spectators were flocking to matches, and Lord's had had the honour of staging the first two Test matches against Australia, in 1884 and 1886. Sir Pelham Warner, writing in 1945,

Right: The second pavilion and A Enclosure during the Eton *v.* Harrow match in 1886, in a painting by Chevallier Tayler.

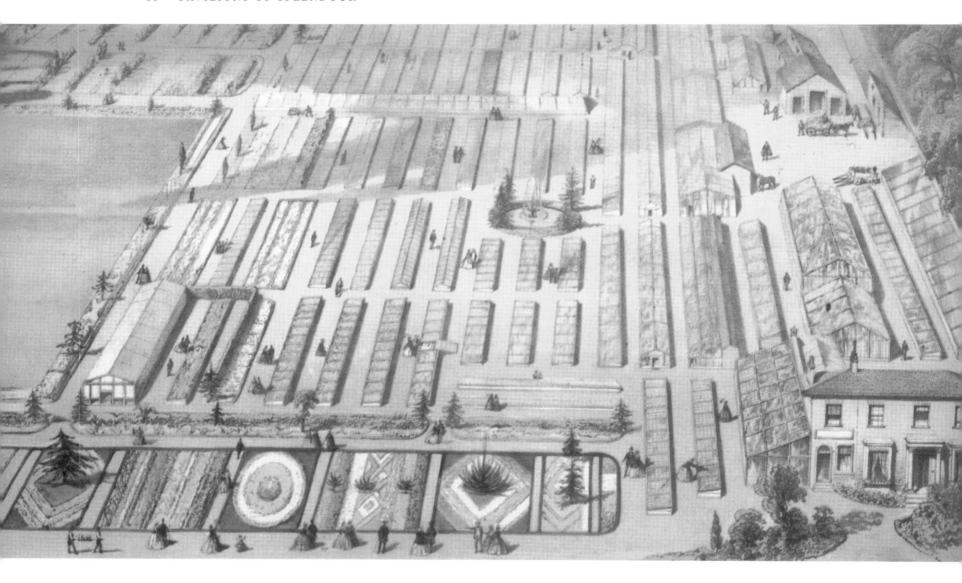

Henderson's Nursery, acquired in 1887, provided the Club with
three-and-a-half acres on which a separate practice area was developed.

recalled with affection his memories of Lord's during MCC's centenary year:

How different was Lord's then from what it is today! Only three buildings remain – Block A, on the left of the pavilion, the hotel and the members' luncheon room . . . There was no big score board or Father Time, the stands were few and small . . . but the atmosphere then was the same as now. Lord's was the home and headquarters of cricket, with a tradition and history which no other ground in the world has ever succeeded in capturing.

The Club marked its centenary by buying Henderson's Nursery from the Clergy Orphan Corporation for the sum of £18,500. This three-and-a-half acre site at the east end of the ground had been a market garden famous for its pineapples (grown under glass) and fine tulips. Its purchase allowed for a separate practice area to be laid; previously, nets had to be erected and removed from the main playing area up to three times a day. The name 'Nursery End' stuck, although today the association is made more readily with the nurturing of young cricketers rather than with fruit and flowers. For a third time the cost was met by a loan from Mr Nicholson, although MCC, not wanting to be too deeply in debt, raised £10,000 from the sale of 100 life memberships at £100 each. The remaining sum was repaid the following year, and at the 1889 AGM the committee was pleased to report that MCC was free of debt.

The Nursery area was further expanded in 1891 when MCC acquired the Clergy Female Orphan School from the Manchester & Sheffield Railway, in exchange for permission to tunnel under the Practice Ground. Members of MCC had for some time been clamouring for a larger and better pavilion, and on 17 September 1889 Sir Spencer Ponsonby-Fane laid the foundation stone of the structure that has come, more than any other, to symbolise MCC and Lord's.

As the century and Victoria's reign drew to a close, MCC's rebuilding programme was almost complete. As Alfred D. Taylor wrote in his 1903 book *Annals of Lord's and History of the MCC*, it took only the building of the Mound Stand, in 1899, to create an aura of authority and complete a magnificent backcloth for the

The ground seen from the pavilion at the turn of the century.

game. This new stand, with accommodation for 10,000 spectators, was constructed on the site of the tennis and racquets courts which, together with numbers 43 and 45 St John's Wood Road, were demolished. Two hundred life members, each paying £200, were elected to finance the project. The Mound Stand was enhanced in 1901 by an iron lattice framework, designed and built by William Slatter, that supported a canvas roof, thus providing shelter from the elements.

The pavilion and
A Enclosure at the
turn of the century.

In sixty years Lord's had been transformed out of all recognition. It was no longer a country meadow but, as Taylor described it in 1903, 'an amphitheatre for gladiatorial contests with its massive and mighty circle of seats, stands, boxes and buildings'. Not all members were entirely pleased with the transformation, but there can be no doubt that MCC was no longer just a private club – it was a national institution. As cricket entered the twentieth century, MCC was the administrative leader of world cricket, and Lord's was a ground that could proudly lead the game into its Golden Age.

That same year the freehold of 3 Grove End Road was purchased, and the site used to build a new tennis and racquets court. This was connected to the pavilion by a bridge over the roadway, thereby allowing tennis members to use the pavilion changing facilities and bathrooms. To meet the wishes of a large number of members, a squash court was also included in the plans.

These two major building projects placed MCC in debt to the tune of £26,000. However, with increased membership (some 9,000 names were on the waiting list) and the administrative capabilities of F. E. Lacey – appointed Secretary in 1897 – the Club was able to balance the books as early as 1904.

In 1900 a refreshment room, complete with seven first-floor private boxes and roof seating for 400, was built next to the luncheon room. A tower was erected to house the clock that had been removed from the old tennis court. It also provided accommodation for a ticket and enquiry office.

3

The Pavilion

1890–2004

The Club's famous Pavilion, home of so much history, is a fine building in its own right. It was built to serve a membership of some 3,600, and continues to fulfil many of its original functions, but now for a membership of 18,000, with not only changing and ancillary rooms, but bars, lounges and cloakrooms, as well as offices for a greatly-increased administrative staff. In addition, it houses some of the key items from the Club's sporting collection – the oldest in the world.

The present building has served as a model for later sports pavilions all over the world, including those at the Oval and Old Trafford. Subsequent additions and extensions have not significantly marred the effect either of the main elevations or of the principal interiors.

In 2001, on the instructions of the Club, Donald Insall Associates and Michael Shippobottom prepared a conservation plan for this wonderful building, the intention being to carry out a study into its present state and to advise upon a strategy for its future. The procedure is one now required by planning authorities, together with English Heritage, in relation to important listed buildings where alteration proposals and continuing change may significantly affect their special character.

The method has a well-defined sequence, and involves close

The main front in 1898.

study of a building both on site and from archive sources, in order to understand fully its historical development and its present form before drawing up headings of significance, issues and future policies. For buildings are like living organisms, subject to constant change yet with continuing and valued identities. Even a building such as the Pavilion is the product now of a long series of alterations – often erroneously assumed to be part of the original fabric. Once its real significance has been defined, areas of lesser quality can be identified, recognising and realising opportunities for future improvement and enhancement. Work on this plan has revealed much new information on the building and permitted the principal interiors to be re-evaluated.

The Architect: Thomas Verity

Speed of construction was a hallmark of the Pavilion's architect, Thomas Verity (1837–91), who achieved fame for his theatre and restaurant work. This included the Criterion Restaurant and Theatre, Piccadilly (1873), the Comedy Theatre, Haymarket (1881) and the Kingsway Theatre, Great Queen Street (1882), in addition to the remodelling of several theatres such as the Empire, Novelty, St James's and Royalty in London.

Verity served his apprenticeship with the National Art Training School in South Kensington, the precursor of the Royal College of Art, where he met former pupils of Alfred Stevens, the great mid-Victorian sculptor. Imbued with the spirit of the Italian Renaissance, he was next sent to Italy to study Italian architecture and the structural use of terracotta. He then assisted Captain Frances Fowke in the erection of the South Kensington Museum, the first part of the Victoria & Albert Museum, and later Lieutenant Colonel H. Y. D. Scott on terracotta detailing at the Royal Albert Hall. Next he won a

limited competition for the Criterion, which established him as a major designer in his own right, particularly of theatres. He became Surveyor of Theatres to the Lord Chamberlain from 1878, and was eventually joined in practice by his son Francis (Frank) Thomas Verity (1867–1937).

He was an early admirer of the New Sculpture movement, which injected a fresh spirit of refinement and sensitivity into decorative sculpture and aimed to integrate it more fully into its architectural setting. His use of robust Neo-Renaissance and Queen Anne styles is characteristic of late Victorian taste, and is seen to good effect at Lord's, while his highly effective planning of theatres on tight sites prompted the Journal of the Royal Institute of British Architects to refer to him in his obituary as being '. . . one of the most skilful planners of the day.' His skill is most evident in his designs for the Criterion, where the auditorium was wholly underground and served by an ingenious ventilation system. His ability to overcome the challenges of a difficult site must have served him well at Lord's, where the Pavilion was built initially hard against the land-boundary.

Because of some later confusion (perhaps introduced by Sir Pelham Warner's 1946 book *Lord's 1787–1945*), the authorship of the Pavilion has sometimes been attributed to Frank Verity rather than to his father – a conundrum which has prompted some writers to take up their pens in attempts to solve the mystery. The evidence, not least that of Thomas's name inscribed on the foundation stone, is however undoubtedly of the Pavilion being his work; and this view was further supported by the discovery during recent research of three original drawings of the building, all of which bear Thomas's name. Nevertheless, given the speed with which the building was designed and erected, and thus the need to use all available skills within the office at the time, it would perhaps be surprising if Frank (who became his partner in 1889) had not taken some part. His contribution would in any case have been obscured by the use of the official practice name on all drawings – a standard procedure in the offices of most Victorian architects.

The building contract for £16,150 was awarded to J. Simpson & Son, a firm of local contractors, a separate specialist contract being placed with J. C. Edwards of Ruabon, North Wales, a well-known firm of terracotta manufacturers. (Edwards's factory in time became the largest in Britain, and supplied much of the decorative terracotta for the buildings on the Cheshire estates of the Duke of Westminster, as well as some of the famous Prudential office buildings designed by Alfred Waterhouse. It is probable that Verity worked with Edwards on other projects, particularly on theatres. Certainly Edwards also supplied terracotta for Verity's elaborate 1887 frontage to 60 Buckingham Gate (now demolished) for Hill's Bakery, as well as for the Kensington Public Baths building of 1889; and when Edwards established his own drawing office, it in turn was run by a Mr Richardson who had been a pupil of Frank Verity.)

It was Frank who in 1891, one year after the opening of the Pavilion, took over the practice, on his father's unexpected death from pneumonia at the age of 53; and it was he who continued to act as architect to MCC, undertaking subsequent alterations within the building itself and notably the reconstruction of the Bowlers' extension. Frank too was a gifted architect. He trained at the Royal Academy Schools in London and then in Paris, where he became much influenced by French neo-classicism, later working on several French-influenced mansion blocks and on the redecoration of the State Apartments at Buckingham Palace.

Thomas died at the end of a sad personal decade, marked by

An engraving of Thomas Verity's design for the Pavilion, 1889. Note the coach and four to left of the picture.

the deaths of two daughters as well as his wife. But his glorious swansong was the Pavilion at Lord's – a building which reveals none of this personal grief and somehow effuses a gentle confidence and assurance of manner – perhaps itself a reflection of his own gentle and assured professionalism.

Bailey's Magazine in 1890 described the new Pavilion as 'really magnificent . . . the building is apparently meant to stand forever . . . it is impossible to count the number of dressing rooms, bathrooms, lavatories etc . . . a grand "Lawcourt of Cricket". It was

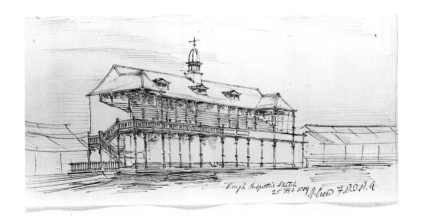

This sketch, dated 25 February 1889, was the unsuccessful submission by Mr R. Creed, FRIBA, for the proposed new pavilion.

built in an era of unprecedented wealth and confidence, and at a time when a relaxed approach to architectural style had become acceptable. Gone was the necessity of working in pure classical or gothic styles: for by now, and certainly for buildings of entertainment, other modes could be embraced.

The main front displays much of the spirit of French neo-classicism, together with detailing influenced by the then-fashionable Queen Anne style. This appears not least in its extensive use of red brick and terracotta, together with white-painted balconies and large areas of plate glass, while vigorous and flamboyant detailing of the terra-

Four of the decorative terracotta heads, allegedly modelled on members of the Committee.

cotta includes the MCC motif together with the Pavilion's construction date of 1890. The row of decorative terracotta heads supporting the consoles of the upper terrace is just one further aspect of this relaxed manner, as well as reflecting Verity's own interest in sculptural decoration. (The heads are said to be modelled on members of the Committee, although the identities of only two have so far been established.)

The external appearance of the building neatly conveys its plan and function, a characteristic like that of the pavilion it replaced. The all-important Long Room and tiered viewing terraces occupy centre stage of the main (east) front, while the twin flanking pavilions (using the word in its architectural sense) reflect their use as committee and writing rooms. Above are the players' two dressing rooms; and each end of the building is served by its own major staircase, expressed in a pair of projecting bays on the entrance (west) front.

Memorable also is the Pavilion's roofline and silhouette – espcially that of the main front roof, whose pitched form with projecting canopies at its northern and southern ends so daintily appears to hover over the building. The resulting lightness is a vital part of the overall design – a lightness emphasised still further by decorative cast-ironwork detailing, very much in the spirit of a seaside pier.

Otherwise the rear of the building comes as a jolt after the lavishness and richness of the main front. It is strictly utilitarian,

built of stock brick and with architectural detail kept to the absolute minimum, the simple sash windows establishing a constant rhythm along the frontage – clearly a case of a Queen Anne front and a Mary Ann behind!

Subsequent Design Changes

From the beginning, successive changes have impinged on the building, first with the addition in 1898–99, on a newly-acquired strip of land immediately west of the Pavilion, of the Tennis Court block. This connects directly across the rear drive onto the Pavilion itself and now appears indistinguishable from it.

Less successful were the alterations undertaken in the late 1930s, which included a mezzanine floor introduced within the southern archway, much reducing its headroom and installing utilitarian windows, all quite at odds with the more generous proportions and fine detailing of the rest of the building. Some hope that this attractive archway might one day be reinstated. Many other changes have been prompted by the ever-increasing demands for improved sight-lines and viewing levels.

These include the replacement of some casement windows on the ground floor by extraordinarily wide sliding sashes. It was a gradual process, beginning with the central casement window of the Committee Room, but here the alteration was considered only a partial success, and the window was subsequently altered again, along with the central casement

window of the Writing Room, where even the terracotta mullions were sacrificed. Vestigial traces of these still survive in their 'shadows' on the lintels. The still-later provision of wide sashes in place of original casements in the Long Room has completed this transformation of some of the key ground-floor windows, introducing at the same time one of the most memorable features of the present building, and one appreciated to the full on a sunny Test match day.

The original terracotta balconies on each end remain, the southern-most one altered at some stage to accommodate a fire-escape link to the adjacent terracing. That in the Members' Bar was enclosed from the 1930s to 2000, and served for part of that time as a commentators' box. The graffiti on its decorative terracotta balustrade are a relic of that period.

Elsewhere two cantilevered balconies were added in 1906 to serve the dressing rooms. A major reconstruction in 1960–61 of the principal first balcony terrace regrettably removed its pretty supporting cast-iron columns with their decorative arms and plinths, as well as the original twin porch balconies of decorative terracotta, complete with their robust supporting columns. Their utilitarian replacement in reinforced concrete, with simple straight balusters at the front, has later been softened by adding a decorative metalwork balustrade, returning to it something closer to its original character.

Beneath the two rooftop-end canopies are further flat roofs originally designed to carry tiered seating, as shown on Verity's working drawing, and at varying times these 'stands' have been put to uses other than members' viewing. The front of the North Stand was enclosed and used as a BBC commentary box from 1972 to 2000, while at the south, a reporters' box was provided. Now that the new Media Centre is in service, both these may now again become available for use by Members.

Adjoining these is the upper terrace built directly over the flat roof of the Long Room. As a result of the fire at the Bradford football stadium, and following the recommendations of the Popplewell Inquiry, earlier timber staging was here rebuilt in the 1990s as a more permanent steel and concrete structure.

The Bowlers' Pavilion

A players' room for use by professionals was initially provided at the north end of the Pavilion in the form of a low extension. This took 'very much of the same pattern externally as the well-remembered rustic Pavilion', noted *Bailey's Magazine* in May 1890. Despite a claim in 1900 that the task would not be feasible, it was extensively rebuilt in 1906 by Frank Verity as the Bowlers' Pavilion, providing further changing facilities and a Press box, whose predecessor across the ground had been blown down in a storm. When at the end of the 1962 season, amateur status for players in the first-class game was abolished, the need for a separate professionals' changing room was removed, though the wing continued in use by the MCC Young Cricketers. It was converted to offices and a bar around 1969–1972, and was again much altered in the 1980s when a new secretariat facility was created at first floor level, projecting out over the rear drive on free-standing columns.

The Allen Stand

The Allen Stand of 1934–35 (formerly Q Stand) was designed by Sir Herbert Baker, in conjunction with the engineer Dr Oscar Faber – a successful early proponent of the use of reinforced concrete. Together they were also working at the same time on the rebuilding of the Bank of England, where beneath a façade of Portland stone there is a complex reinforced concrete structure.

The Allen Stand is perhaps one of Baker's lesser works, witheringly dismissed by Sir Pelham Warner as 'devoid of architectural merit'. The connection to the south side of the Pavilion was effected by a simple footbridge, which thus involved minimal alteration to the Pavilion's south façade, but it did intrude on the terracotta decoration, necessitating some removal of original detail, as well as internally subdividing the first floor Dressing Room in order to create an access-corridor.

Interiors

The principal floor comprises a series of handsome public rooms overlooking the field to the east and centred on the famous Long Room. These main rooms are arranged enfilade, with glazed connecting doors permitting a view along the full length of the building. This arrangement ensures the transparency and openness so favourably commented on at the time of construction: 'There is no "secret chamber", for the Committee Room is simply divided from the centre room by two glass swing-doors, and this is the case with the library and writing room also.'

Serving primarily as viewing galleries from which to watch matches, these also provide for use as committee and general meeting rooms, reading areas and a formal dining room. Together with the Long Room Bar and Old Library, they form the core of the building, which with the two stairs integrates into the rest of the Pavilion.

Above all and at their heart is the justly famous Long Room – extending to ninety-three feet – its length reflecting that of a traditional long gallery in a medieval country house, but with a much greater ceiling-height. This is a truly special room whose charged atmosphere is created as much by its architecture as by the impact of the intensely green field outside, a proximity heightened by the virtually fully-glazed wall. The architecture of its Queen Anne detailing provides a background at once dignified without being austere, and with a character which is

The North Stair today, showing the Second World War memorial on the landing and a typical elaborate overdoor to the Old Library adjacent.

The glazed connecting doors from the Long Room to the Writing Room.

generous and comfortable while introducing tension with the hard flooring and lack of soft furnishings such as curtains. How much more dignified the room must have looked with its original elaborate fireplace-surrounds and overmantels and a ceiling divided up by a richly-patterned design, before these were all swept away in the 1950s.

The Long Room continues to be as much used – and as much loved – as it ever has been in its century of life. It has provided an appropriate setting for some of the greatest cricketing occasions, in addition to MCC's annual Christmas Dinners. But there can have been few moments as dramatic as that in the 1945 game between England and the Dominions, when one of Hammond's sixes shot into the room and hit a display case.

Of only slightly less significance are the Committee Room and Writing Room, which together with the Long Room and inter-vening halls form the enfilade facing the playing area. Like the Long Room, these have not only witnessed the great games of the past but have hosted some of the great discussions and presentations of cricketing history. In the Committee Room for example the South African and MCC teams were presented to King George VI in 1951, and Field-Marshal Montgomery was welcomed in 1945. Robust and dignified Queen Anne detailing is continued throughout the two rooms, with panelled pilasters and Corinthian capitals supporting the ceiling downstand beams, all echoed in a simple painted dado below. These two rooms alone retain their fireplaces, which originally would have been a feature of all the larger rooms in the building. The glazed and panelled doors, together with their ornate overdoors, are a striking feature of these interiors; and, not surprisingly in view of Verity's work elsewhere, are eloquently reminiscent of late Victorian theatres. Many of them carry good original or early ironmongery,

The Long Room as it appears today.

Top: The Long Room in about 1914.

Centre: The Committee Room in 2004.

Bottom: The Writing Room in 2004.

including decorative door-pulls and robust doorknobs, hinges and locks. Yet although most of these doors and overdoors have survived intact, the doorway connecting the Long Room with the Long Room Bar has regrettably been blocked to create precious display-space.

To the west and rear of the Long Room are the former Library and Bar – further major rooms, high-ceilinged and again with robust, even lavish architectural detail reflecting their special importance. Below them, the basement or lower ground floor is reserved for members' cloakrooms and for more office accommodation, together with services and storage. These utilitarian rooms have lower ceilings and simple finishes; and although some of their uses are known to have changed, the basement has probably always served for similar functions, although an observer in 1890 enthused tantalisingly that 'the cellars are a sight in themselves'. Perhaps this was referring to the generous coal stores and coal-fired boiler room – or was it to the Secretary's wine cellar?

The first floor is dominated by the dressing rooms for the two teams; and their forward siting permits an uninterrupted view of the pitch and the awaiting crowds. Along with the dressing rooms are ancillary dressing, bath and shower rooms and physiotherapy suites. At the second floor, the building is capped on the north by Players' and Committee Dining Rooms, and on the south by further offices and a Members' Bar and Lounge.

With every space testifying to some incident in cricketing history, and occupying such a central part in cricketing lore, this is a building which can be altered only at some peril. Nevertheless, as in nature, all buildings need to adapt to change, and to respond to new circumstances. It is perhaps a reflection of how well the Pavilion was designed initially that it has proved so

The Old Library with stair to the Bowlers' Bar on the left.

readily capable of such adaptation over the last century. Some necessary improvements have included the tactful insertion of a lift in the 1990s and the provision of women's cloakrooms. More will undoubtedly need to be done in the future, as sensitively as possible, and perhaps some of the building's original features may be restored in the process.

In the Long Room, for example, early photographs indicate (in contrast to the present scheme) dark, probably grained joinery, although a lighter colour was adopted for the pilasters; and by the time of a 1937 photograph the dado, originally plain, had clearly received a panelled treatment. The darker-coloured joinery treatment also extended at least to the doors of the staircases, as the 1937 photograph of the Long Room reveals a dark reverse side of one of the stair doors which is shown open.

A photograph taken in about 1953 intriguingly also shows the decorative treatment within the field of each ceiling panel of the Long Room, a feature described as 'old figured ceiling-paper, which gave the impression of having been there since the Pavilion was built in 1889'. Such treatment was not uncommon in interiors of the 1890s and particularly those in the 'Queen Anne' or 'Aesthetic' taste fashionable at the time - parodied so notably by Gilbert and Sullivan in *Patience*. But it was a style quite out of fashion in the clean-cut, utilitarian era of the 1950s, when, after some discussion on whether it was possible to clean the ceiling, it was stripped off and in its place plain soffits were introduced with 'stripes of cream and rich Indian red . . . to pick out the mouldings of the ceiling panels and relieve the rather sombre tones of the celadon walls'. This was all part of a comprehensive decorative scheme designed by architect Louis de Soissons and undertaken at a cost of £1,100. At some stage in the 1970s the present green colour scheme was adopted.

The Long Room in 1937.

From the photographic evidence it seems that the other principal ground floor rooms were also originally decorated in richer and darker colours than now. The 1939 photographs of the Committee Room and Writing Room clearly show wood graining on the main defining architectural elements, including pilasters, dado and windows. Similar treatment would almost certainly have been applied to doors, although none appears in the photographs. Indeed it may be assumed that a consistent or related scheme was adopted in the enfilade of all the rooms flanking the pitch and throughout at least the ground floor.

Elsewhere in the building, light-green colour schemes were in general use throughout the 1970s – perhaps the same as were retained in the Long Room. Wallpaper, such as that in the second floor Members' Lounge and Bar, has been introduced into the Pavilion only comparatively recently.

Structure and Services

The structure of the building is deceptively simple, no doubt for ease of procurement and above all for speed of construction. There are traditional strip footings and load-bearing masonry walls; and the floors are on timber joists and steels, with sound-absorbent 'pugging' in the more sensitive locations. Services also were relatively straightforward at first, although they now display a century of change and enhancement. The heating, by a hot water system, was served initially by a coal-fired boiler situated probably in the basement room where the present Club Office is now housed. Heating of the other main rooms was by coal fires, laboriously fed from a coal store down in the basement. Some of the cast-iron column radiators remain; and these are of two distinct patterns, one with a slightly Art Deco character clearly betraying its later origin.

Given Verity's progressive interest in electric lighting, as in his Alexandra Theatre of 1881 and his Green Park Club of 1891, it is possible the Pavilion may have been lit by electricity from the first; but the only record so far found is of 1899 and refers to electric fittings being installed in both the Pavilion and Tennis and Racquets Courts for '£74, including fittings, extra lights to be supplied where necessary, pro-rata'. This early date may however be compared with Cragside in Northumberland, the first private house to be lit by electricity, which dates from 1880–81. The House of Lords was converted to electric lighting in 1882. The Royal Academy of Arts installed electric lighting for an exhibition in 1882 and in all its galleries by 1893.

Photographic evidence of lighting in the Pavilion interiors before 1939 is seemingly restricted to the Long Room. Here a 1914 photograph clearly shows suspended bowl fittings, one to each main bay of the ceiling, and similar to a pattern patented by Holophane in 1909. Perhaps it was artistic licence which omitted these pendants from Hanslip Fletcher's sketch of 1949; but they are featured in Dennis Flanders' drawing of 1953, and were replaced with more modish fittings in the dramatic redecoration of the room in 1954. By the time the National Monuments Record photographed the room in 1981, even these fittings had been removed, and each large painting is shown individually illuminated by a picture-light – presumably augmented by lights within the two recessed showcases. An upstand above the main cornice had at this stage been added, housing the concealed striplights that today provide uplighting.

Furnishings and Memorabilia

The robust oak tables in the Long Room, Committee Room and

Writing Room all appear in the earliest photographs and are probably original; but the high oak spectator chairs which are such a feature of the Long Room are a comparatively modern replacement of the original heavier versions, at least one of which survives in the Museum.

Oak cabinets in the Writing Room and the war memorials in the hallways are again key elements in the historically significant furnishings. Lord's is justly celebrated not only for the famous urn containing the Ashes, but also for its unique collection of cricketing memorabilia, comprising not merely bats and caps, cups and glasses, but also a superb display of prints, photographs and paintings. Many of these are on show in the Museum; but some special items, including certain of the most important historic paintings, are hung in the Pavilion. There are frequently recurring themes, such as the historic aerial photographs on the south stair, while on the north stair are displayed mainly prints and paintings of public-school cricket and a collection of evocative early views of Lord's.

A detailed plan to conserve, restore and upgrade the fabric of the Pavilion, both externally and internally, was approved by the Committee in April 2003. Members approved the project at the AGM on 5 May 2004. At a cost of some £8.2 million the works will restore the historic parts of the building such as the Long Room to their original Victorian designs. The turrets will be returned to members' use as viewing platforms, and a new roof terrace will be created behind the present upper terrace. All the rooms, including members' areas, players' facilities and staff offices, will be modernised and redecorated. The work began in September 2004.

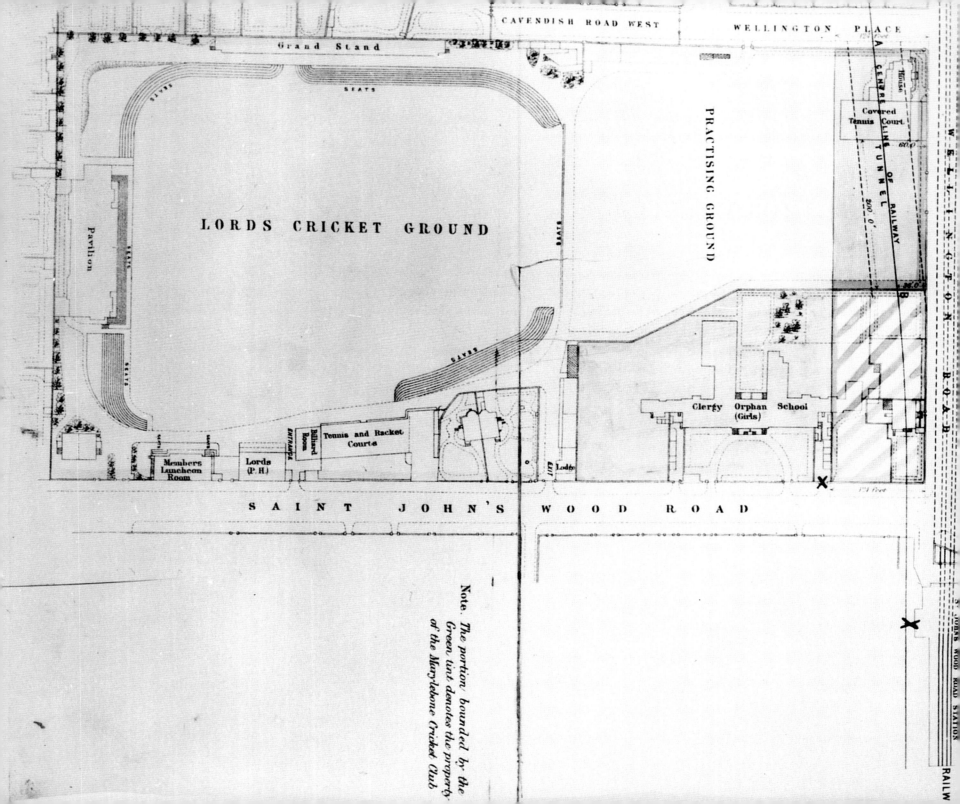

CAVENDISH ROAD WEST   WELLINGTON PLACE

Grand Stand

House

Covered
Tennis Court.

PRACTISING GROUND

LORDS CRICKET GROUND

W E L L I N G T O N   R O A D

CENTRE LINE OF RAILWAY

TUNNEL

SEATS

SEATS

SEATS

Pavilion

SEATS

SEATS

Clergy Orphan School
(Girls)

Tennis and Racket
Courts

Billiard
Room

ENTRANCE

Members
Luncheon
Room

Lords
(P. H.)

Lodge

EXIT

✕

S A I N T   J O H N ' S   W O O D   R O A D

Note. The portion bounded by the
Green tint denotes the property
of the Marylebone Cricket Club

✕

ST JOHNS WOOD ROAD STATION

RAILW

4

The Railway Threat

1890–99

In 1890 MCC was thrown into turmoil when the Manchester, Sheffield & Lincolnshire Railway (later the Great Central Railway) proposed a bill in Parliament to construct an extension of its line into the newly built Marylebone Station.

The Bill posed a real threat to Lord's, as the proposed new line would have resulted in the compulsory purchase of large chunks of the Nursery Ground –which MCC had just acquired at some cost in 1887.

MCC was adamant that this should not take place and the Club's annoyance was expressed in a letter dated 11 December 1890 from Mr C. Liddell, a railway engineer, to Mr W. Pollitt of the railway company:

> Mr Perkins [Secretary of MCC] . . . explained his determination to oppose the line to the utmost . . . the committee have paid £25,000 for three-and-a-half acres of the nursery ground and they don't want to sell any part . . . and will do their utmost to prevent the Manchester, Sheffield & Lincolnshire Company taking a foot of their ground. In short he is irreconcilable.

MCC had plenty of local support. The proposed construction

was very unpopular with many well-known and influential residents of St John's Wood whose protests were similar to those made a hundred years later by the residents of Kent against the introduction of high speed trains through the Garden of England. On 11 December, a public meeting was held in the newly-built Pavilion at Lord's to protest against the proposed scheme. Mr Seager Hunt, MP, chaired the meeting and a veritable army of artists, cricketers, lawyers, churchmen and local politicians voiced their opposition to the plans of the railway company.

Pollitt went on behalf of the railway company to a meeting with the MCC Secretary. In a memorandum dated 16 December 1890, now in the Public Record Office. Pollitt reported that 'Mr Perkins expressed himself very strongly against the slightest interference with the cricket ground'. Perkins explained that MCC had for many years been improving their position at Lord's and, being now in possession of a freehold property that had cost the club some £100,000, it was not prepared to forego any part of the property. MCC was not a profit-making company – its only

Top:
Lord's *v.* the railways:
a contemporary
cartoon.

Bottom:
Tunnelling on the
Nursery Ground
in 1896.

LORD'S IN DANGER.   THE M.C.C. GO OUT TO MEET THE ENEMY.

["Sir EDWARD WATKIN proposes to construct a Railway passing through Lord's Cricket Ground."]

object being to provide the finest cricket for its members and the general public.

The following month Perkins wrote a letter to all secretaries of cricket and other clubs in London, in which he expressed his objections to the 'wanton and unnecessary interference with Lord's'. The railway company officials replied with their arguments for the scheme in a letter that appeared in *The Times* on 30 January 1891.

The two sides had reached an impasse. MCC was intransigent in its opposition to any proposal that resulted in the loss of part of its ground. Equally the railway company was determined to provide the public with another railway terminus in London – Marylebone Station.

Obviously a compromise was needed, and the first signs of one emerging came in a letter sent on 11 February 1891 by S. Bircham, solicitor to MCC, to Sir Theodore Martin who represented the railway company. In this letter Bircham indicated that MCC had been offered a piece of ground from the Clergy Orphan School (situated adjacent to the Nursery Ground) which was double the area that the railway company wished to acquire. He also outlined the conditions under which MCC would grant the railway company access to Lord's provided that this land were obtained for the Club. That same day Sir Theodore himself wrote to the railway engineer, Liddell, 'Herewith I send a copy of the terms stipulated by the Lord's people. They are very stiff, but I fear they will stand to them.'

News of the dispute between MCC and the railway company had already reached the press and, although on 11 February the *Manchester Courier* hinted that the warring parties were close to a settlement, it did not hesitate to add its own opinions to the debate. The newspaper's view was that the inhabitants of St John's

Wood had been 'left in the lurch by the cricketers' – it also felt that the 'working classes of Marylebone' would 'welcome the idea of a great railway terminus in the district'.

That same day the *Manchester Examiner* noted that Sir Henry James, MP (a former President of MCC) would not move the rejection of the Railway Bill in Parliament. Then on 24 February the *Pall Mall Gazette* added fuel to the fire by reporting that, despite claims to the contrary, the Clergy Orphan Corporation was not prepared to negotiate the sale of its land to the railway company.

On 6 April MCC held a special meeting at which the options open to the Club were debated. The dispute rumbled on throughout the summer and feelings were still running high at another special meeting held on 8 December. It was evident that opinions among the membership were divided, although by now the MCC Committee was practically unanimous in its total opposition to the Bill unless land could be obtained in compensation.

The influence that a number of prominent MCC members and St John's Wood residents were able to bring to bear in important Government circles eventually proved too much for the railway company. Bircham was relentless in his lobbying of MPs on MCC's behalf and in a letter dated 11 December 1890 was able to report that 'Royal Assent will not be given to it (the Railway Bill) unless the clause for the protection of the MCC as agreed forms part of the Bill.'

Eventually, MCC received the specific protection it sought in Clause 3 of Section 52 of the Extension to London Act 1893.

After this, matters proceeded amicably and the agreement reached was a satisfactory one for all concerned. The Clergy Orphanage land was incorporated into Lord's and the children relocated to new homes in the country. The railway company was allowed to tunnel under the practice ground on the agreement that, once the work had been completed, the ground surface would be completely restored.

Tunnelling work began in August 1896 and was completed in April 1898 to the Club's total satisfaction. Marylebone Station was the last great railway terminus to be built and the inaugural train service began in March 1899, almost a decade after the controversy had begun.

5

The Grace Gates

1919–23

Dr W. G. Grace died on 23 October 1915. He lived through what has come to be regarded as cricket's Golden Age, the conclusion of which was marked by the Great War and his own death. In an appreciation written for *The Times*, Sir Arthur Conan Doyle concluded: 'Those who knew him will never look at the classic sward of Lord's without an occasional vision of the great cricketer. He was, and will remain, the very impersonation of cricket.'

It was inevitable that the Committee of MCC would wish to commemorate the Doctor, and it was equally predictable that there would be much debate as to how this should be done. The President attended his funeral, and at the next Committee meeting it was decided to consider the creation of a memorial: 'A desire was expressed to recognise the late Dr W. G. Grace's eminence as a cricketer in a memorial, but it was felt that the present was not the time to carry the wish into effect'. At about the same time the Committee received reports of the sale of geese on the ground at eleven shillings each, and the purchase of lambs for spring feeding.

It is not clear what led the Committee to turn to Herbert Baker for advice in preference to Frank Verity, who had been the

W. G. Grace wearing his MCC cap,
by Alfred Bryan.

Club's architect since the death of his father. Perhaps one consideration was that Verity's practice had been badly affected by the war: indeed, it had suffered to such an extent that in 1920 he was declared bankrupt. He was, nevertheless, retained by the Club to design new workshops, which still stand on the north side of the Practice Ground. They consist of three units, a single-storey brick forge between two-storey brick-and-tile buildings. The eastern one, with its iron balcony, remains a workshop; the other, with the clock tower, is used as offices by the International Cricket Council.

There is a clue to the reasons for Baker's appointment in his autobiography, *Architecture and Personalities*. He was born and brought up in Kent, and refers to cricket as his favourite pastime. His father's agricultural estate was close to Cobham Hall, the home of Ivo Bligh, who captained the first official team to go to Australia in 1882–83 (the side played three Test matches and recovered the Ashes). Bligh was in his prime when Baker was a boy – and many years later Baker designed the memorial for Bligh's grave in Cobham. In his teens Baker captained the Tonbridge School eleven, and later he was elected to the Kent Club 'The Band of Brothers' when Lord Harris was leading the County's cricket. When, in 1919, MCC finally decided to create a Grace memorial, Harris had just been elected to succeed Sir Spencer Ponsonby-Fane as Honorary Treasurer, and it was he who consulted Baker for suggestions.

Another link between Baker and Harris was Cecil Rhodes, the architect's first and most famous client. When, in 1885, Harris returned from India, where he had been Governor of Bombay, he not only picked up the threads of his cricketing life, but began a significant career in the City of London. He joined the boards of a number of companies, and became Chairman of Consolidated Goldfields, which had been founded by Rhodes. Furthermore, Cecil's brother Frank had played cricket with Harris in the Eton XI, and had been his military secretary in Bombay.

Sir Herbert Baker's professional life was interwoven to a remarkable degree with that of Sir Edwin Lutyens. Between 1887, when Lutyens arrived at the office of Ernest George & Peto, where Baker was the senior of two assistants, and the death of Lutyens on New Year's Day 1944, they were in turn friends, partners in the great enterprise of building New Delhi, bitterly alienated by disagreements over money and designs, estranged colleagues in the creation of memorials to the dead of the Great War, professional rivals and towards the end of their lives friends once more. Both designed many fine houses and a number of important public buildings. Lutyens was the greatest architect of his generation, but Baker secured more prestigious public projects by being more politically sensitive.

As a boy Baker had failed his entrance examination to Haileybury, apparently because of his ignorance of Classics. He seems to have felt this keenly, and throughout his working life never missed an opportunity to decorate his buildings with Latin or Greek inscriptions. There were other paradoxes. He developed a convoluted style of writing that incorporated frequent quotations of poetry, but stressed his lack of literary skill. He referred in his autobiography to his intellectual shortcomings, but nevertheless tried to write about philosophy and what he called 'creative and spiritual art.'

Lutyens's biographers refer to Baker as being 'tall, idealistic and priggish', someone who 'revered the public school ethic of team spirit, was a Christian idealist and a great reader of poetry'. It was said that he always carried a volume of Wordsworth in his pocket.

Baker pleaded modesty, but he was far from lacking in self-

Herbert Baker,
MCC's architect for
over thirty years.

Johannesburg and Pretoria. It was Rhodes, with his love of Greek and Roman architecture, who pointed Baker towards Classicism, and by sending him to study the buildings of the ancient world made him in effect the first Rhodes scholar.

Baker was high-minded, and his work in South Africa, his lectures and articles, placed him in the forefront of British contemporaries. In one article he drew an analogy between architecture and British imperial rule. He often quoted Wren's dictum that architecture has its political use: 'It establishes a Nation . . . makes people love their native Country, which Passion is the original of all great Actions in the Commonwealth.'

When he was approached by MCC in 1919, Baker's reputation was in the ascendant. Already famous for his work in South Africa, and his collaboration with Lutyens in New Delhi, he was at this time absorbed with work for the War Graves Commission. He designed the memorials at Neuve Chapelle and Delville Wood, at Haileybury and Reed's Schools, and the Memorial Hall at Winchester College.

At Lord's he concluded that the best position for a memorial would be in the space between the stands at the far end of the Match Ground, directly opposite the Pavilion. He proposed a wall enclosing or supporting a bust of Grace on a plinth overlooking the field. This could be the first of other monuments that might be added, so as to create what he called a *campo sancto* for heroes of the national game.

This idea was turned down. Lord Harris tried to be tactful, saying, 'The Committee quite appreciate the charm of your suggestion, but they consider that it does so much interfere with cricket that they could not recommend it'. The trouble was that it would have obstructed the access for rollers to the playing area. Baker reckoned this a poor excuse, around which a way

confidence. The trigger that sent him to South Africa in 1892, at the age of thirty, was the fact that his brother Lionel, who had preceded him there, wanted their father to invest money in a small fruit farm. 'It was an anxious decision for my parents to take,' Baker wrote. 'At their suggestion I agreed to go out to the Cape to report, and to advise my brother about his plantation venture.'

Soon after arriving in Cape Town he had the great good fortune to be asked by Cecil Rhodes to refurbish the house he had just bought. This was the start of an increasingly close relationship, which continued until Rhodes's death in 1902 and led to Baker designing many major buildings in Cape Town, could be found, but to no avail. The Committee at that point thought it would be better to put a bust of W. G. beneath an open-sided stone canopy on the raised grass area behind what was then A Block (now the Warner Stand).

After meeting Harris at Lord's, Baker sent a sketch of how this idea might be executed, insisting that 'our hero must be placed at a height from which he can watch the game: a privilege you must not deprive him of.' For the second time his suggestion was rejected. The Committee had changed its mind about the financing, and as a consequence the location, of the memorial.

The original intention had been for the Club to bear the cost. Now, while still guaranteeing the whole, the Committee proposed that a subscription list be opened so that up to half the cost could be contributed by 'cricket clubs and admirers of the late Dr Grace'. Therefore, it was argued, the memorial should not be enclosed within the ground, but open to public view. Harris wrote to say that the Committee wished the memorial to be in the form of a gateway, which he was authorised to ask Baker to design.

Baker accepted that the gateway might be a better idea than his second suggestion, 'though certainly not of [sic] the first'. Indeed, so wholly was he convinced of the merits of his first idea that he could not bear to let it drop. He risked incurring the wrath of the Committee in two ways. In 1914, when house-hunting, he had by chance met Pelham Warner, while looking at Warner's house, and now, on 9 December 1920, he wrote to him canvassing support for the first idea. On the following day he sent Francis Lacey, Secretary of MCC, two new drawings. One was of the gateway, the second a simplified version of his first scheme.

The long delay between July 1919, when Baker was originally instructed to prepare a design, and December 1920, when the drawing was submitted, was due to the fact that the architect spent time in India, and on his return was extremely busy. There was a further delay until the beginning of July 1921, when Harris wrote to Baker to say that the Grace Memorial Sub-Committee had, owing to the Chairman's ill health, been slow in getting down to work, but now wished to interview him to discuss progress with the gates. Harris said also that it had again turned down Baker's first idea. 'I have done my best as regards your designs, much preferring the first, but to no purpose.' This was reiterated firmly when Baker met the Sub-Committee at Lord's on 12 July. The Committee wanted a double gate with an inscription on a central pier, but no bust, and possibly pedestrian gates at the sides.

Accepting defeat, Baker decided to set the gates back from the line of the red-brick boundary wall, and to build three piers in white stone. The two outer piers, each capped with a decorative urn, would be connected to the boundary walls beside them by curved white stone walls, with a doorway in each. The central pier, more massive than those to each side, would be finished with more ornate carving, and would bear an inscription.

In each opening he set a pair of iron gates, of which he wrote in his autobiography: 'On the ironwork of these gates I put a symbol of the game, a red ball surrounded by the golden rays of the sun; an idea taken from E. V. Lucas's poem, 'The Cricket Ball Sings', in his *Open Road*:

> Shine in the hearts of my cricketers, shine . . .
> Heroes, bow all to the little red ball,
> And bow to my brother ball blazing on high.

The gates were made by the Bromsgrove Guild, which had been established in 1898 by the management committee of the Bromsgrove School of Arts. The guild was designed to capitalise

on the contemporary demand for high-quality workmanship in metal-casting and wood-carving, and at the same time to provide much-needed employment for the young people of the town. In 1905 the Guild had been commissioned to provide the huge cast-iron railings and gates for the remodelled forecourt of Buckingham Palace, together with the Great Gates of Canada, the Australian Screens, and the rest of the metalwork that surrounds the Victoria Memorial.

With the Grace gates, MCC wanted quite extensive ancillary works. These included the demolition of some buildings to the left of the new entrance, and re-positioning of the ladies' and men's cloakrooms. Baker was also to provide an extension to the covered lunch-room in place of a tent. In tackling this brief he suggested, not untypically, the expensive option of putting the men's lavatories underground, but the additional cost of £1,500 was too much for the Committee, and he was asked to modify the scheme.

By the middle of October 1921 the matter had progressed sufficiently for the Secretary of MCC to write to Baker to say that, except for a few details, his designs were approved, and he was authorised to obtain tenders for the cost of carrying out the work.

It is at this time that the name of Charles St Leger first appears in correspondence. Then an assistant to Baker, St Leger became the member of his staff principally responsible for work at Lord's for nearly twenty years. Curiously he gets no mention in the architect's autobiography.

By 22 December 1921 tenders had been received from six building companies, all within the remarkably small compass of £700. The Committee accepted the cheapest, submitted by J. Carmichael (Contractors) Ltd, in the sum of £11,209. Of this £2,268 was for the memorial gateway and £8,941 for the ancillary

Left: The gates as viewed from the road.

Right: Detail showing the symbol that appears on each of the four gates.

works. The Annual Report in May 1922 commented that 'It will be a satisfaction to the members to know that a large proportion of the amount has been spent in finding employment at a time when it is so much needed.'

It was, perhaps, a sign of the times that work started on 28 December, only six days, including Christmas, after acceptance of the tender. It was completed in June 1922, and on 20 July the President, Lord Chelmsford, wrote to extend praise and thanks both to Baker and to St Leger for their work on the memorial and the new luncheon accommodation. Grace's widow was invited to open the gates formally, but declined. Carmichael had to wait until May of the following year for the Committee to approve their final account, which included an additional £791 3s 3d on the recommendation of the architects, whose fees of six per cent of the total were also approved.

Even more sensitive than the architectural design of the memorial was the wording of the inscription. After much debate in committee and the receipt of suggestions by others, the question was finally solved by Sir Stanley Jackson, who said, 'Why not simply "The Great Cricketer"?' So the inscription reads:

TO THE

MEMORY OF

WILLIAM GILBERT

GRACE

THE GREAT CRICKETER

1848–1915

THESE GATES WERE

ERECTED BY THE MCC

AND OTHER FRIENDS

AND ADMIRERS

The Memorial being decorated to commemorate the fiftieth anniversary of the death of W. G. Grace.

Two postscripts are worthy of mention. In December 1939 Baker's advice was sought because the stonework of the Memorial had weathered and become discoloured, and some of the arrises and mouldings and part of the carving had started to flake. The architect expressed surprise, since the best quality Portland stone had been used, and he considered that the damage must have been caused by sulphur from smoke in the atmosphere: 'The two large power stations in the vicinity are not helpful'. His advice was that the stone should be washed with clean water from a fine spray, using a fibre brush, on a warm day when there was no danger of frost.

In 1966, at the start of the redevelopment of the south-western corner of the ground, the gateway had to be taken down and rebuilt thirteen feet to the east of its original position, to make way for the new Tavern and members' dining room.

Block A running
from north of the
Pavilion round to the
original Grand Stand.

6

Three New Stands

1923–26

At the end of the First World War, as Herbert Baker began his association with MCC, a continuous sweep of roof extended over the few rows of seats that ran from the north end of the Pavilion around the north side of the ground to the sight-screen at what is now called the Nursery End. The arc in the north-west corner was known as Block A. The seats here dated from 1874, the time when the playing area was raised and re-levelled. Three rows of fixed seats had been installed for the public, and this number had increased as the years went by. The roof then covered seats in front of the 1867 Grand Stand, which stood back behind the road running at the back of Blocks A, B and C, with its rear wall on the line of the northern boundary of the ground.

The southern half of the ground presented a more interesting appearance. Immediately south of the Pavilion was a small stand, with its higher rows of seats under cover. Formerly known as Block D, it became Block Q when the stands were renamed in 1924. Between this and the western end of the Mound Stand was an open area in front of four buildings which backed on to St John's Wood Road. The oldest of these was the Lord's Hotel, renamed in 1951 as the Tavern. Brick-built on three floors, and dating from 1868, this stood where a tavern had existed since Thomas Lord purchased a lease of the ground in 1813. Against its western wall was a small building, from the front of which was sold confectionery baked on the premises.

On the west side of the shop was the Members' Dining Room, built in 1881, with its roof occupied by a bank of seats called Block O. Adjoining this building, and linking it to the clock tower that stood behind Block D, was the Members' Dining Room extension. Built in 1898, it contained, on the ground floor, a refreshment room, on the first floor seven boxes, and on the roof seating for some 400 people, designated Block P. In the same year as it went up, the original tennis courts were pulled down, together with numbers 43 and 45 St John's Wood Road, to make way for the

Mound Stand, which curved round the south-east corner of the ground from the Tavern to the Nursery End sight-screen.

Such were the seating arrangements in 1919.

At a poorly-attended meeting of the Committee of MCC at Lord's in the afternoon of 11 August 1921, Lieutenant Colonel F. H. Browning proposed that a special sub-committee be set up to examine, inter alia,

1. The Grace Memorial Gates.
2. Increasing the Mound Stand.
3. The desirability or otherwise of putting up hard lawn tennis courts on the Practice Ground.
4. Rebuilding and alteration of the Grand Stand.
5. Possible purchase of houses and land.

It was decided that a sub-committee should be convened as soon

The original Grand Stand, completed in 1867.

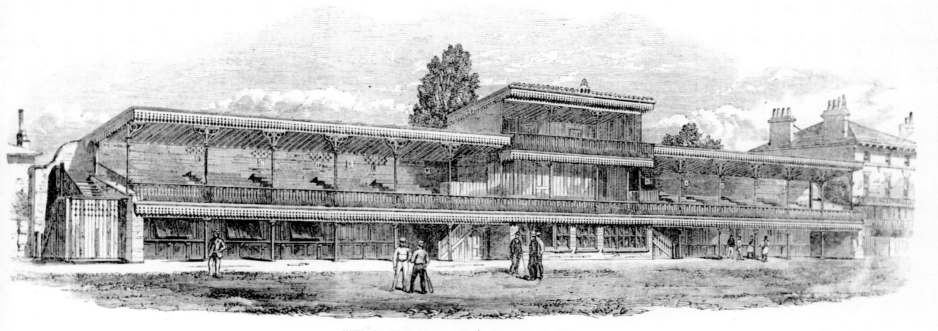

NEW GRAND STAND, LORD'S CRICKET-GROUND.

as possible after the holidays – but neither the proposer of the motion nor his fellow members can have been very wide awake. At the next meeting the Treasurer had to remind members that there was already in existence a Grace Memorial Sub-Committee. He could have said also that the Property & Works Sub-Committee had already in March that year examined plans for increasing stand capacity in response to mounting pressure from members

on a report and plans for increasing stand accommodation. These were considered at a joint meeting of the Property & Works and the Arts & Decorations Sub-Committees on 30 November 1921, with Hull in attendance. He recommended that the Grand Stand be pulled down and a new stand erected in its place, giving an increase of about 2,500 seats at a cost estimated at between £20,000 and £30,000. The Treasurer did not approve of this, stating that he was

Left: Blocks A and B seen running in front of the original Grand Stand.

Right: The Clock Tower and original Block Q in the 1920s.

and the public for more accommodation and better facilities. Mr P. W. Hull, MICE, had attended its meetings and explained various alternatives, 'but had not recommended the adoption of any.' In recognition of his services, the Committee had agreed to send Hull a complimentary ticket for the 1921 season. It is difficult to imagine Herbert Baker being either so reticent in offering an opinion, or content with a free pass for his work!

After the inconclusive discussion in March 1921, Hull set to work

not prepared to admit the necessity for a new stand at the present time, as he considered it would be possible to extend the existing Grand Stand without incurring 'so great an expense'.

Nevertheless, the Committee provisionally approved the proposal, but before making a final recommendation authorised the Secretary to enquire whether the Eyre Estate would sell a portion of the garden of 29 Cavendish Road. This, together with a strip of land taken from the gardens of 12, 14, 18, 20, and 22 Elm

Tree Road, which were owned by the Club (there was no number 16), would have enabled a new road to be created behind the proposed stand, which could then have been built over the existing roadway.

The Annual Report of May 1922 referred to the work of Mr Hull, and noted that the Committee had decided to defer further consideration. No further reference to Hull appears in the Club

records, and nothing happened for nearly a year, until on 12 March 1923 the Property & Works Sub-Committee reported that at its last meeting a proposal had been carried that 'Herbert Baker, ARA, be asked to visit Lord's and discuss the practicability of increasing stand accommodation'. (In 1922, to the dismay of his great rival and one-time partner, Edwin Lutyens, Baker had been elected an Associate of the Royal Academy). The success of his Grace Memorial, completed the previous June, was bearing fruit,

and he now found himself engaged to build three major stands, a type of structure of which he had no previous experience.

A meeting with the President and Lord Hawke, Chairman of the Sub-Committee, was arranged, and letters were exchanged about fees. These were, it was decided, to be settled by the President at between £50 and £100. The President came off second-best in this negotiation, as the fee was agreed at 100 guineas for a report only, with no sketch designs 'worked out in any detail' and nothing more than 'the roughest estimates'.

Baker defined his purpose as being to increase the number of seats and to 'dignify the amphitheatre'. His proposal was to add an upper tier on the whole of the north side of the ground – that is, above Blocks A, B, and C and the Grand Stand, where he included two tiers of boxes, grouped in the centre and at the ends. There was also a suggestion that boxes might be added 'above the stands opposite the Pavilion'. By this Baker intended that the new upper tier over Block C could be terminated with boxes under a tiled roof, and similar boxes could be built on the other side of the gap, above the northern end of the Mound Stand, so that from the Pavilion there would be a symmetrical outlook. Baker calculated that his plans would in all provide 5,764 extra seats at a probable cost of £44,000, which included rebuilding the Grand Stand.

Charles St Leger, Baker's assistant, attended combined meetings of the Finance and the Property & Works Sub-Committees on 18 and 23 July 1923. He explained that the plan was divided into five separate schemes. These were described to the Committee on 30 July, and the minute reads as follows:

> Scheme 1: (Block A) to provide 1,000 extra seats to cost about £4,000.

Inset: The south-west corner of the ground seen in 1938 in this picture by Charles Cundall showing, from left, the Mound Stand, the Scoreboard, the Lord's Hotel, the Members' Dining Room, the Members' Dining Room Extension, the Clock Tower, Block Q and the Pavilion.

Scheme 2: (Old Grand Stand) to provide 2,000 more seats to
cost about £29,000.

Scheme 3: (Block B) to provide 1,500 more seats to cost about
£6,000.

Scheme 4: (Block C) to provide 647 more seats to cost about
£2,500.

Scheme 5: (Large Mound Stand) to provide 650 extra seats to
cost about £2,500.

The Sub-Committee decided to postpone decisions on Schemes 1, 2, and 5, and to recommend adopting Schemes 3 and 4, 'minus the box'. The Secretary was instructed to ask St Leger if Scheme 1 could be modified to provide additional seats without obstructing the view of play from carriages, and to explore ways in which additional seating could be provided in Schemes 4 (without adding too much to the height) and 5.

Revised plans, with rough estimates, were sent in before the July Committee meeting. In a covering letter Baker expressed surprise that the Committee should consider it worth sacrificing 1,000 extra seats simply to preserve the view from carriages. He proposed a significant extension of the Mound Stand, as well as of Blocks B and C. In the absence of St Leger to explain the plans in more detail, it was decided to postpone deliberations.

At a Finance Sub-Committee meeting in August it was decided to proceed with Schemes 3 and 4, without the 'pavilions', but with additional seating on the south end of Block C. It was hoped that building could begin in October 1923, but this proved optimistic and it was not until December that the President was authorised to accept the tender of either Trollope & Colls at £7,940 or Holloway Brothers at £8,045, depending on the advice of Baker. He opted for the lower.

The contract provided for the removal of existing seats, the building of a new lower curve of terraced seats, and the construction of a cantilevered upper deck in reinforced concrete. When St Leger pressed for the appointment of a clerk of works to oversee the reinforced concrete work, at a weekly wage of four guineas, the Committee asked for an explanation as to whose interests the clerk would protect. Once reassured that it would be those of the Club, it gave agreement.

The January start brought problems. A railway strike severely disrupted the work, and prolonged frost caused further loss of time. At one point the District Surveyor stopped the work because of the cold, and after this the concrete had to be heated and extra centring used in order to avoid a longer hiatus. When completed in April 1924, the new stand covered the north-east arc of the ground, between the east end of the Grand Stand and the sight-screen.

By the end of April early problems were reported: rainwater was seeping through the expansion joints. The first remedy suggested by Baker, the fitting of iron guttering beneath the joints, was not a success. Baker then enlisted the help of a structural engineer, Dr Oscar Faber, who advised that a simple remedy would be to apply 'special concrete paint' to the upper surface of the joints. The Committee asked Baker who would pay the estimated £12 cost, and accepted his opinion that it should be the Club. It was included in Trollope & Colls' final account when that was eventually settled on 9 January 1925 at £8,445 2s 2d. Another extra was the amount claimed for the time lost due to frost.

In August 1924 Viscount Ullswater (President, 1923) submitted a sketch and suggestion for further seats. His plan was to add an upper tier at the north end of the Mound Stand, and was a modification of Baker's original Scheme 5, taking into account what had actually been built on the north side of the gap. St Leger gap. St Leger explained to the Sub-Committee that if an upper deck was to be added to this part of the stand, it would be advisable to lower the existing ground-level seats so that they matched those 'on the north side of the gap by the bowlers' screen'. He estimated that the scheme would add about 1,000 seats and cost about £8,000. The Sub-Committee liked the plan and the uniformity it provided; but, having noted also that the cost of each extra seat would be double that of the last contract, postponed a decision until the next season.

At the Annual General Meeting on 6 May 1925 the President, Lord Ernle, referred to Baker's plans for the Ullswater proposal, and for rebuilding the Grand Stand. The latter, he said, raised 'problems of finance for which solutions had not yet been found'. Nevertheless, after further discussions the Committee agreed in principle to proceed with Baker's Scheme 1 (seating over Block A) and Scheme 2 (rebuilding the Grand Stand) as well as the Ullswater plan. However, no more was heard of Scheme 1.

A Special General Meeting of members was convened for 13 July 1925. Two resolutions asked those present to approve 'the increase of seating accommodation both for members and the public', and to empower the Committee to elect, in priority of entry, 200 candidates at £200 each as life members. The members, after a long discussion and some opposition, approved both with the majority prescribed by the rules.

In response to an enquiry from St Leger, the Committee decided that preparation for the new stands could begin on 2 September 1925, and that only British Empire materials should be used in the construction. On 12 and 29 August Baker attended meetings of the Property & Works Sub-Committee with Faber. They were well aware of the tension in the minds of Committee members, for keenness to progress with the new buildings was tempered by anxiety as to whether the work would be completed for the next season's visit by an Australian touring team.

Baker and Faber advocated taking a 'short cut' in two ways. First, by dealing with the new seats at the north end of the Mound Stand before they tackled the Grand Stand, they could use the skilled labour for seven instead of four months. They assured the meeting that the work would be finished before the next season, and that the contractors would agree to a penalty clause in the contract. Baker then submitted a tender of £8,573 from Trollope & Colls for this new stand. His advice to start with this work was accepted, as was the tender. Second, he suggested that there should be a departure from the normal procurement procedure for the Grand Stand, by obtaining from Trollope & Colls a tender based on a bill of quantities and a negotiated schedule of prices.

At the second meeting of the Sub-Committee Baker and Faber were supported by St Leger, Mr Horder, the quantity surveyor, and Mr Elliott of Trollope & Colls. The previous day Baker had written to the Secretary, Francis Lacey, to say that 'by working at high pressure and the denial of holidays' he had done more than anticipated, but not enough to obtain competitive tenders in the traditional way. In fact he had diverted on to this task all seven assistants from his Bank of England work, and it was Horder and Faber who had sacrificed their holidays.

He reminded the Secretary that Trollope & Colls had won a tender two years earlier, for the construction of the new stand in the north east corner of the ground, and again he referred to the pressure imposed by the need to finish the work by 1 May 1926. Baker tightened the screw further by enclosing a copy of a letter from Trollope & Colls, in which the builders stressed the difficulty of meeting the timetable, and asked that the completion date for the back rooms in the Grand Stand be extended to 15 May. This

was an important date, as MCC was due to begin its match against the Australian tourists on the following day.

The Sub-Committee thought the letter displayed 'some apprehension', and the Treasurer opened the meeting on 29 August by reminding Baker that in this contract time had always been of the essence, and that he had given an assurance before the Special Meeting of members that had approved the project. This Baker now repeated, although he thought some fitting-out might not be finished. In case this happened, he asked for an extension to 15 May. The penalty clause would oblige the contractor to pay liquidated damages of £100 for every week or part of a week during which the work remained unfinished beyond that date.

Elliott raised the question of night work, saying that while he hoped it would not be necessary, if it had to be used, the cost would be added to the contract. He suggested also that, 'with a view to getting the best out of the workmen', the Club should set aside free seats for them in certain matches. No decision was taken about how night work should be treated, but the workmen were promised their tickets.

The Committee then considered a tender for the Grand Stand from Trollope & Colls of £36,000. Baker admitted that a competitor might tender a lower bid, but he stressed that he might not be able to give the same assurance about completion on time. No contractor, he said, had a higher reputation 'especially for getting work of this kind through quickly and well, and very often on a trust basis of Prime Cost'. He told the Committee that it had to decide whether or not it was preferable to employ a contractor with previous experience of this type of job, who would in any case be working on the other new stand. To seek other tenders would inevitably delay the start of work, and the Club would run the risk of another contractor competing for the labour available.

A considerable debate ensued. The minutes say that 'the pros and cons were most carefully and seriously discussed, every possible objection being advanced'. Much weight was given to the fact that the Sub-Committee had been impressed by the evident intention of the experts to get the work done to time 'as a matter of honour'. Also, Faber had provided reassurance by saying that he had made a liberal allowance for time that might be lost through bad weather and 'the procrastination of the [London] County Council'. The Treasurer undertook to write to the LCC to

Demolition of the original Grand Stand in progress in 1925.

Foundations of the second cantilever stand with part of the Mound Stand in the background (1925).

press for urgent consideration of the plans. After some hesitation the Committee instructed Baker to proceed, and thus Trollope & Colls were able to work on the necessary demolition and construction of both stands at the same time.

Soon, however, there came another indication that Baker was not experienced in designing this kind of structure. Two years earlier he had been asked to raise the height of the upper deck on the first cantilever stand, but those sitting in all except the first few rows below still had a very restricted view of anything much above ground level. The same disadvantage was shared by the stand to the north of the Mound Stand.

Now he had to apologise for the fact that there would be fewer seats than planned in the open part of the Grand Stand because it had been found necessary to construct the cantilevers above the stand, whereas he had drawn them underneath to show a clear surface above.

Construction proceeded apace through the winter, but in April Alex Scott, from Baker's office, had to attend a Committee meeting to try to deal with the problem that the central boxes were obstructing the view from a number of seats. It was decided to adopt a partial remedy of cutting away brickwork at the sides of the boxes.

Three weeks later Scott was back with worse news, this time not of Baker's making. When the Committee met at Lord's on the afternoon of 5 May 1926, Scott confirmed what members would have seen with their own eyes as they entered the ground. In consequence of the General Strike, which had begun that day, all building had stopped. Subject to certain work being done by the MCC's own staff, he thought that part of the Grand Stand could nevertheless be used on 16 May, but both he and the builders pointed out the risks of such action.

The main outstanding tasks were to clear away building materials, plant and rubbish, and fix barriers and railings to the satisfaction of the District Surveyor. In spite of the warnings, the Sub-Committee advocated that this should be done, but there was clearly some anxiety about possible repercussions. Trollope & Colls raised the question of extra insurance to cover damage due to riots. The Committee did not think this necessary, but did decide to engage two additional night-watchmen at the rate of one shilling an hour. They were not needed for long. The General Strike was short-lived and ended on 12 May.

As it happened, the start of the MCC match against the Australian tourists was delayed because of the soft state of the ground, and there were frequent interruptions for bad light and rain before the game was abandoned. However, the new Grand Stand and balcony, and the cantilever stand at the north end of the Mound Stand, were both finished in time for the Test match which began on 26 June. In contrast to the earlier game, the weather was splendid on all three days. Such was the interest in the match that the gates had to be closed on the Saturday, and the attendance over the three days was 72,976.

Compared to its predecessor, a handsome red brick building but with very limited accommodation, the new Grand Stand must have appeared huge. Its reinforced concrete terracing was supported by a mixture of structural brickwork and reinforced concrete, and it had a pitched roof of Italian tiles. The lower tier of seats matched those of the cantilever stand to its east, and extended back to the original road that had run in front of the old stand.

Above the rear rows of these seats Baker put a deep balcony, again matching the upper tier of the stand to the east. Continuing up behind the balcony was a bank of covered seats which bridged

Sir Herbert Baker's Grand Stand seen
with a capacity crowd in the mid-1960s.

the roadway. At each end of the stand were lower and upper boxes, and two levels of boxes were put each side of the central scoreboard, above which was the scorers' accommodation. Dining rooms built at upper levels behind the seats, and boxes were approached by a complicated arrangement of staircases, which shared the north side of the road with a new printing room, a restaurant and a bar.

The Old Father Time weather vane, which became to many the symbol of Lord's, was a gift to MCC from Baker, and was, apparently, a complete surprise to the Club. It is about 6ft 6 ins tall in total, with the figure itself around 5ft 4ins, and is made of cast iron, painted black with gilding on the tip of the wind-arrow and the end of the sickle. The figure represents the mythical Father Time who watches over the passage of the years. There has long been debate as to whether he is placing the bails at the start of a game or removing them at the close of play. J. H. Fingleton, the Australian player and author, and Diana Rait Kerr, MCC's first Curator, both suggested the latter, but E. W. Swanton took the more optimistic view that the bails are being placed in anticipation of a day's cricket.

There remained the matter of Baker's fees and the builder's final account. As far back as August 1925, when the Committee had considered the appointment of Trollope & Colls, Baker had said that he thought his usual fee of six per cent, which he would share equally with Faber, would not remunerate him adequately. He hoped that the Committee would sanction seven or seven-and-a-half per cent. The Committee said it would consider the request when work had been completed. On 7 June 1926 Baker wrote to the Secretary to confirm that the fee for all three stands, had indeed seemed meagre. He and Faber had shared £3,209, which he did not consider enough. On 27 July Lacey was able to

The Old Father Time weather vane in its original position atop Sir Herbert Baker's Grand Stand.

offer Baker a further £500, which he accepted with alacrity, writing by return of post to express his thanks, and saying, 'It will not have been a very remunerative job for me, but I am only too glad to render some service to Lord's'.

Trollope & Colls submitted final accounts in July 1927. For 'erecting a concrete gallery and reconstructing the lower seating adjoining the Mound Stand' the account was £8,362, against a contract sum of £8,459. For the demolition of the old stand and re-erecting the Grand Stand, the account was £38,053 – this time, slightly more than the contract sum of £36,591.

In reporting these figures to the Committee, Baker said that he understood that the contractors would make a further claim, outside the terms of the contract, for an extra payment in consequence of 'the exceptional difficulties under which the work had been done'. Faber, in a separate letter, stated that the contractors faced a large loss. The Committee referred the question to the Finance Sub-Committee, which took its time to review further correspondence from Baker, and from Trollope & Colls. The contractors said that their net loss was £3,856, due to the need for night work in order to finish on time. Delay had been caused by a short rail strike, a period of exceptionally bad weather and 'ferment among labour just before the great strike'.

In December the Committee accepted that MCC should bear half the loss, subject to Baker verifying the contractor's figures. At the next meeting it accepted a recommendation from the Finance Sub-Committee that the Club should pay £1,500 of the loss – a decision which seemed to please everyone.

Was the Grand Stand a building of which MCC and Baker could be proud? In May 1926 the Committee decided that 'Mr Baker should be informed that the appearance of the stand is quite suitable', and two meetings later offered him, St Leger and Scott seats on the balcony for the Test match. The Annual Report prepared for the AGM of 1927 said that 'the view obtained from these [new] seats, except in the case of a few seats in the corners of the Grand Stand, gave, it is believed, general satisfaction'.

This reference, and the willingness of the Committee to consider favourably Baker's request for an extra fee, are of interest. Pelham Warner's criticism that the structural arrangements behind the balcony (from which he admits the view was magnificent) were badly designed, with a maze of staircases and with some seats affording less than a full view of the cricket, had some justification. His acid comment that 'Never in the history of cricket has so large a stand held so few people' is often quoted, but dissatisfaction with restricted views of the playing area seems in truth to have grown up only slowly.

In a retrospective survey of the previous thirty years, published in *Wisden* in 1930, Lacey referred to the Grand Stand without criticism. E. W. Swanton said of it in his essay 'The Mecca', one of a collection published in 1977 under the title *Follow On*:

> It is greatly in its favour that it has dignity, and blends well with the Pavilion. On the other hand, considering its size it gives a satisfactory field of view to the minimum number. Some seats are unsaleable, since from them can be seen only one set of stumps. At its rear is a honeycomb of stairs and passages, and some of the dining rooms are situated in bizarre relation to the boxes they were designed to serve . . . There is at least a splendid view from the balcony.

The LCC monitored the continuing safety of stands by regarding them as temporary structures licensed for a period of years, and subjected then to close inspection on the expiry of every term.

The first cantilever stand had been licensed initially for a year but then, together with its twin to the south of the sightscreen and the Grand Stand balcony, was licensed for five years. In 1932 the MCC had to pay £228 for waterproofing, and at various later times its own labour force was engaged in trying to correct problems caused by reinforcing steel-work being too close to the surface of the concrete, which led to the concrete breaking away and exposing the metal.

In 1937 the Secretary wrote to Baker to say that the District Surveyor had just renewed the licence for the Grand Stand balcony and the stairs and upper tiers of the cantilever stands, on condition that defects of the same nature were made good. This was reported immediately to Faber, who inspected the stands and wrote at some length on 10 May. He thought the structures were in excellent condition, considering that they had been exposed to the weather for some ten years with practically no expenditure on them. It was his view that the work required to be done was certainly no more than normal for buildings of this character after that length of time. He produced an interesting calculation comparing interest on the capital cost of the stands at five per cent with the amount that the club had spent on maintenance, apart from decoration, which he calculated at about one per cent. Thus he reasoned, the stands had been a good investment. Faber concluded his letter by stating:

> For the benefit of the members of the committee who were not members when the stands were under construction, and are not aware of the circumstances under which the stands were erected. The order was placed about Christmas and the stands had to be ready at the end of April, a total of four months out of which the plans were awaiting the approval of the LCC for

The first cantilever stand (completed April 1924), seen in winter.

three weeks. The work was delayed by heavy and continued frosts and strikes. This made the completion of the stands in time before the Australians were due a miracle, and this will no doubt be taken into account when criticism of the workmanship which in a few instances is not perfect, is made.

Baker was alarmed at this aggressive response, and wrote to Faber:

> I think it would be wise and politic if you revised your attitude. I think the Committee would be much more lenient to what was certainly a fault in supervision if we frankly admitted it, while we emphasised the fact that your method of construction was approved by the District Engineer; that it could not be done otherwise; and that we had all the difficulties to contend with of an unsatisfactory contractor, bad workmen, bad weather and pressure of time. We are much less likely to put their backs up by taking a reasonable attitude, and it would be more diplomatic on your part in view of the similar work that we hope we will undertake there.

Faber took this reproach in good part and replied, 'I am very grateful and will with pleasure amend my letter to incorporate the improvements you suggest. They improve the letter very much.'

Baker was right. On 13 May he wrote to Faber to say that he and his assistant Victor Helbing had attended a meeting at Lord's (which would have been with the Property & Works Sub-Committee) and went on:

> I am sorry to say that we came in for very severe criticism – generally that the design was wrong if faults that have shown themselves are due to bad centering and insufficient thickness of concrete. We shall have to be careful how we handle this situation. The whole affair is rather disturbing and it is difficult to convince these people who, being laymen, cannot understand the technical details.

Faber was disappointed that he had not been summoned to the meeting. Whether this was the choice of the sub-committee, or because Baker and his partner Scott felt, in view of Faber's aggressive attitude, that it would be impolitic, is not clear. Faber denied that the design was bad, and pointed out that on the relevant drawing he had put a large note in red directing that all rods were to have a cover of concrete of not less than one inch or the diameter of the rod, whichever was the greater, with the exception of the half-inch rods in stairs and slabs, on which the cover must be not less than half an inch. This had, he said, been agreed with the technical expert at the LCC and was in accordance with the best advice and opinion of the time, and in accordance with the regulations. He admitted that it now appeared that the contractors had not in all places provided the cover required by the design, thus tacitly agreeing with Baker's admission that there had been a fault in supervision.

He reiterated the problems caused by the need to give all spectators adequate sight-lines, and reminded Baker that this was one of the first cantilever stands ever constructed. He dealt at length with criticism of the design of the expansion joints, and of the level of fees paid, and went on to advise as to how the stands should be dealt with. He concluded by suggesting that if the committee agreed to proceed as he suggested, either Holloway Brothers or Peter Lind should be approached to do the work.

At its meeting on 19 May 1937, having considered a letter from Baker and Scott and Faber's report, the Committee decided to accept his recommendations and to obtain quotations from Holloway Brothers and Peter Lind on a specification drawn up by Baker.

When, in 1995, preparations were being made to apply for planning permission to demolish the Baker Grand Stand, and replace it with the Nicholas Grimshaw design, there was some anxiety about the reaction of the Planning Authority. It was therefore decided to commission a report from Anthony Blee, FRIBA, FRSA, on the existing building.

Blee dealt with the impact on the ground, and on the Conservation Area of St John's Wood, of the demolition of the Baker building and the Grimshaw replacement. While mentioning Baker's awards and major achievements, he compared him unfavourably to Lutyens, and said, in relation to his work at the Bank of England, that his 'dastardly devastation on Soane's original masterpiece will never be forgiven'. He was reinforcing comment by H. S. Goodhart-Rendell that Baker's work at the Bank was 'an outrage, incongruous and ignorant'.

Warming to his theme, Blee then quoted other critics. Kenneth Clark had said that Baker had 'a positive genius for errors in design', while A. B. Knapp-Fisher maintained that his major work in London 'reveals his limitations'. Goodhart-Rendell, apparently known for his acerbic comments, in an interview with Nikolaus

Pevsner had only one comment on Baker: 'Such a bad architect'. On the other hand, Blee reported that Pevsner thought the Grace Gates 'excellent', and said of the Grand Stand that it was 'large but low key, with somewhat oppressive lower parts'

Blee also quoted Viscount Chelmsford, the former Viceroy of India and President of MCC, who said that Baker was 'always up to time and within his estimate', which reputation, together with the mark of esteem denoted by election as an ARA, caused MCC to ask him to make the Grand Stand design 'a severe test and a trial of ability. But anybody who has been to Lord's can see how an architect of real distinction can invest a building of utilitarian purposes with dignity and beauty'.

In summary, however, Blee was right in saying that the facilities of the Grand Stand were elementary, and the servicing too cramped, while Oscar Faber's engineering embodied no technological innovation or achievement in its own right. Now, he reported in 1995, it could be seen to have been vulnerable to progressive deterioration of a kind that was irreversible. He concluded that the Grand Stand was not an important example of the architectural opus of Sir Herbert Baker, but an elementary composition with no specific historic interest: 'Baker loved his cricket, but he was not in his element when he came to design for Lord's.'

7

Staff Flats and Arbours

1928–37

The staff flats, completed in March 1929.

Three months after the final accounts for the new Grand Stand had been settled, and the extra fee for Herbert Baker – now Sir Herbert – had been paid, MCC asked his assistant, Charles St

Leger, to prepare alternative schemes for building two or three staff flats on the north side of the ground between the workshops and the north gate.

On 26 April 1928 St Leger sent the Secretary a sketch for three apartments, one each on ground, first and second floors. The block faced south, overlooking the Practice Ground, with its back hard up against the northern boundary of the ground on Cavendish Road. The plans were considered by the Property & Works Sub-Committee on 8 June 1928, and its recommendation to proceed was accepted ten days later, subject to some alterations. The most fundamental was to change the original design of white, rendered walls above a brick plinth, and a slate roof, to red-brick walls and a tiled roof. Second, the ceiling heights were to be nine feet, and last, all rooms were to be heated by gas and lit by electricity, with coin meters for both. This decision was altered as building work neared completion, and open fireplaces were provided in the sitting-rooms. Subsequently, the Committee directed that the bricks to be used should be similar to those used for the new buildings by the members' entrance, and of British manufacture.

On 1 October 1928 St Leger reported the receipt of three tenders, the lowest being from C. Miskin & Sons of St Albans, in the sum of £4,175. This was accepted on condition that the contract would be completed in twenty weeks.

The block has nine-inch, solid brick walls under a roof which is partly tiled and partly lead-covered. The plainness of the south-facing front wall is relieved by two bays on each floor. The windows give the impression of being rather small and were

originally metal casements. These have been replaced in recent years by plastic-framed, double-glazed units.

The roof is complicated. Instead of using a central ridge with plain front and rear facing slopes, it was designed with a main ridge set towards the front, and a rearward projection at each end. Thus the steeply-pitched tiled slopes are in plan the shape of an elongated 'U', and the space between the rear extensions is a lead flat. This arose from the Committee's preference for a tiled rather than a slate roof, which could have been laid to a shallower pitch. Baker explained this to the Secretary: 'We made this piece of flat roof because if the roof were built of tiles the steep pitch entailed a very high roof, which is wasteful and too dominant.'

The ground-floor flat is smaller than the two above, because of the need to provide stairs to the upper floors, and has four rooms, a kitchen, a small bathroom and a toilet. by the back door off the kitchen. The first- and second-floor flats have five rooms, a kitchen and a bathroom.

The apartments were completed at the end of March 1929, and the rents for the employees who occupied them were set at a nominal ten shillings per week. In July the builder's final account was settled at £4,339 11s 6d. In March 1931 it was reported to the Committee that the flats were damp owing to condensation. This was overcome by dry-lining the walls, and estimates were sought for the installation of a low-pressure combined water-heating apparatus.

Although all the correspondence was with St Leger, it is impossible to imagine that Baker did not have some influence on the design of the building. Again the Club seems to have presented him with a new challenge. In South Africa he had designed many grand houses and very few workers' cottages, most notably those in the village of Languedoc, for Rhodes Fruit Farms. In New Delhi

his share of the work had included some residential buildings, but these had been heavily criticised by Lutyens: 'Slovenly and capricious, especially the bungalows (bungle-ohs)'. Their quarrel over the gradient to the Viceroy's House in New Delhi, and their subsequent disagreement about the design of a Memorial for the Imperial War Graves Commission, no doubt made Lutyens a far from unbiased critic, but workmen's accommodation was not Baker's forte.

The flats remain, although altered a good deal internally. Modern kitchens and bathrooms and gas-fired central heating have been installed – but the ground staff who occupy them pay considerably more in rent than did the original tenants. Although the rooms are small, the accommodation is comfortable, and to any lover of cricket the situation is incomparable.

The decision in 1928 to build the flats was not an entirely new departure. For a long time small rooms on the second floor of the hotel on the St John's Wood Road frontage of the ground had been set aside for staff occupation. When Baker's senior assistant, Victor Helbing, made a survey of the hotel in June 1937, he found that the accommodation on the second floor, which was occupied by staff, consisted of five small rooms overlooking the ground and four overlooking St John's Wood Road, with one bathroom and two WCs.

Helbing's visit was occasioned by the Committee's wish to examine the feasibility of building a new hotel on the corner of St John's Wood Road and Grove End Road, on land that had been part of the garden of 2 Grove End Road. Half the site of the house had been used for luncheon rooms when the Grace Gates were built, and the house had been demolished soon after, leaving the rest of the land empty. Now the idea was that a new hotel could provide either two or four staff flats on the second floor.

Although the plans came to nothing and the war intervened, the need for more staff accommodation remained in the minds of Committee members.

In March 1944 Alex Scott had a discussion about the future with the General Purposes Sub-Committee. It was emphasised that some staff flats were still needed, but there was no agreement about where they should be situated. At another meeting in May the Committee seems to have endorsed, without enthusiasm, Scott's suggestion that they might go on the northern edge of the ground. In June Colonel H. A. Henson, the Deputy Assistant Secretary, wrote to Scott to say that the Club required four families to be accommodated – but two weeks later the architect had to inform Henson that the completion of his plans would be delayed as his office had suffered bomb damage.

On 2 August the plans were finished and revealed an imaginative proposal. Scott's idea was to replicate the existing block of three flats and connect the new building to the original one by a two-storey link containing the fourth flat on the first floor, above a new entrance to the ground on its northern side. In the middle of the month the General Purposes Sub-Committee approved the scheme in principle, but asked for open fireplaces to be provided in each of the living-rooms.

In July 1945 the plans were finally recommended for approval, and Scott advised that he did not anticipate a delay in getting a licence for the construction. His confidence appears to have been misplaced, because the flats were never built. Even so, in August 1947 he submitted an account for a fee of three per cent of Higgs & Hill's tender price of £14,590.

Years later, in 1964, a small, square detached house on two floors, its walls of brick up to first-floor level and tile-hung above, was erected where Scott had intended to build the flats. It remains to this day, housing one family where the Club could have accommodated four.

The Arbours

On 24 October 1929 a severe gale caused extensive damage to a number of the arbours, or open-fronted shelters, with roofs of corrugated iron supported by timber frames, which had for many years enclosed the Practice Ground on its north (Wellington Place), east (Wellington Road) and south (St John's Wood Road) sides. These had been used since 1903 by members for luncheon on major match days, principally Test matches, Gentlemen *v.* Players, Oxford *v.* Cambridge and Eton *v.* Harrow. The Committee had them built because of its concern at the damage done to the turf of the Match Ground by large tents used at these society functions. They were equipped with sinks, benches and cupboards and a supply of gas and water. The gale must have been of extraordinary ferocity, because debris from the wreckage was alleged to have caused damage to the roof of Christ Church, Marylebone, some distance away.

The professional advice of Dr Oscar Faber was that the arbours which remained standing were in a dangerous condition. Indeed, it was his opinion that all had been unsafe from the moment they were built. The total weight of the construction was only 6 lb per square foot, including the concrete blocks in which the feet of the posts were bedded. The Building Act required structures to be designed for a wind pressure of 25 lb per square foot.

Faber wanted to be sure that his clients understood his message:

> If ever a considerable wind should be exerted against the front of

The first arbours seen in the distance on the far side of the Nursery Ground before the First World War.

these arbours . . . it would lift the whole structure up and deposit it in some adjoining place . . . Portions of the roof might be thrown on to traffic in the surrounding streets and the Committee would, I fear, become liable for any damage that would result.

Understandably, the Committee took the drastic decision to rebuild all the arbours, and St Leger presented plans to the meeting on 2 December 1929. He proposed to replace the old structures on the same layout as before: that is, with ten backing on to Wellington Place, one in the corner of Wellington Place and Wellington Road, twenty-nine backing on to Wellington Road, one in the corner of Wellington Road and St John's Wood Road, and seventeen backing on to St John's Wood Road. The structure would be reinforced concrete piers and roof trusses, with a corrugated asbestos roof. The estimated cost was £4,250, which excluded some items that it was thought 'might be necessary'. These were guttering and rain water pipes (£400), drainage for the rainwater (£360) and tar paving under the arbours (£740 if laid on existing foundations and £1,440 if new concrete foundations were needed).

The Committee was very keen to get the work completed before the next season, and followed the precedent set when the Grand Stand was rebuilt. The contract was not put out to tender, but St Leger was told to instruct Holloway Brothers Ltd 'on the basis of agreed current rates'.

There is no record of why Holloways were chosen. They had tendered unsuccessfully for the Grace Memorial Gates, and were narrowly beaten in tendering for the first cantilever stand to the east of the Grand Stand. However, Baker thought highly of the firm, which was his main contractor in the rebuilding of the Bank of England.

St Leger attended the first meeting of the Committee in 1930, together with a Surveyor, Mr C. A. Robertson, to report a major problem that had been encountered with LCC. The back wall of the existing arbours on the eastern boundary formed the boundary with Wellington Road. Now the LCC was insisting that the back wall of the arbours should be built twenty feet in from the boundary wall. Mr Robertson stated that the LCC might be prepared, as a special case, to reduce the building line to ten feet, but only on conditions that would outweigh any advantage to the Club. He hoped it would be possible to obtain a licence to build a temporary structure up to the wall. However, in view of plans for road-widening, the licence would be for five years only. Robertson reported also that the cost of rounding off the corner of St John's Wood Road and Wellington Road, suggested by the LCC, which would involve the Club in moving its boundary wall and altering its plans to omit the arbours in that corner, could form the basis of a compensation claim.

For the arbours that would back on to the Wellington Road, St Leger proposed to form the frames from cast-iron members, bolted together, so that if the building had to be moved at a later date, it could be shifted without destroying the structure. The roof would be of corrugated asbestos sheeting on steel purlins. The revised estimate of cost for the main work was £4,496, with additions for renewal of the tar paving (£713), drainage (£490), new gas and water services (£330), plus 'an amount to be settled later for providing facilities for boiling water'.

The Committee accepted the plan and confirmed its instruction to appoint Holloway Brothers on the same basis as before. It decided that Baker and the engineer, Dr Faber, should share equally a fee of eight per cent of the total cost. But on the next day, 7 January 1930, the Secretary wrote belatedly to St Leger to inform

Aerial view of the ground in about 1958 showing the arbours around the Nursery Ground.

him that under the terms of the lease by which the Club occupied this part of the ground, no structure could be built, since 'the surface is ours to a depth of 18 inches only'.

At the meeting of the Committee on 3 February 1930 the Treasurer (Lord Harris) reported that the restriction in the lease followed a similar clause in the Act which had authorised the compulsory acquisition of the land for the construction of the railway tunnels. The Surveyor of the London North Eastern Railway Company had confirmed that the Company had no objection, despite the terms of the lease, to MCC rebuilding the arbours. Harris felt that to proceed in these circumstances would leave the Club 'at the mercy of a common informer'. He advised that rebuilding should await the outcome of the Railway Company's petition to amend the Act by repealing the provision forbidding building on the land.

The Committee accepted the position, agreed to defer rebuilding, and instructed the Secretary to arrange for canvas covering to be provided for the Oxford & Cambridge and Eton & Harrow matches in 1930. Baker and Faber were concerned that the delay could be substantial, and applied for £85 each, representing two per cent of the estimated cost of the new arbours, it being understood that this would be regarded as fees on account if the scheme went ahead on the basis of work done to date, but not if a new plan had to be devised.

Nineteen of the original arbours had survived the gale, and the Committee decided to take the risk of retaining them for use during the 1930 season. It sold the old corrugated-iron roofing from the others for £10. Mr Robertson continued his discussions with the LCC throughout the early part of the summer. At the last meeting of the Committee before the summer recess it was agreed to defer a decision as to whether the arbours along St John's Wood Road and Wellington Place should be built, and to leave the framework for the canvas in place throughout the winter.

St Leger's plans, drawn in July 1930 in readiness for a two-stage reconstruction, include a section which shows the foundations for the walls of the Wellington Road arbours as being eighteen inches deep, and eight feet above the top of the roof of the railway tunnel.

During the first few days of September 1930 the Secretary was informed that the petition to amend the Manchester, Sheffield & Lincolnshire Railway Act 1893 had been successful: the clause which forbade building on the company's land had been repealed. During the negotiations, however, the railway company had been obliged to give up to the London County Council a strip ten feet wide of their land fronting Wellington Road. This was, of course, part of the land leased by MCC. Robertson pointed out the inevitable to William Findlay, the Secretary. In a letter dated 10 October 1930 he advised proceeding with the new arbours against the north and south walls, 'as it is now quite definite that the Club will not be permitted to erect any structure within ten feet of the present wall'.

St Leger considered this good advice and revised his plans, omitting the corner arbours. The quantity surveyors priced the cost of the nine eighteen-foot bays along Wellington Place and the sixteen similar ones backing on to St John's Wood Road, at £3,239. On 13 October, at its first meeting after the summer recess, the Committee authorised this rebuilding. St Leger suggested that, as the new Wellington Road arbours would have steel frames, the same form of construction should be used for the rest. The Committee disagreed, for some inexplicable reason preferring the reinforced concrete frames, but told St Leger to see that the fronts harmonised. In November the Committee accepted a tender from Holloways of £3,228 16s 5d, subject to the LCC giving consent to the re-building.

By the end of the year formal agreement had been reached with the London & North Eastern Railway Company on the conditions which would apply if consent for the rebuilding of the arbours was given. If the Company had to repair or renew the tunnels, and the work involved coming onto the surface, the Club would, at its own expense, have to remove the buildings temporarily to facilitate access.

In February 1931 there was good and bad news for the Committee. The Secretary reported that oral permission had been given by the LCC for work to begin on the Wellington Place and St John's Wood Road arbours, and that in consequence Holloway Brothers had started work on 26 January. Baker, however, had been informed in writing by the Council that work should not begin before the boundary wall at the corner of St John's Wood Road and Wellington Road had been splayed, and the land 'added to the public way without compensation'. The St Marylebone Borough Council had undertaken to rebuild the wall at the corner and, moreover, offered £76 in the settlement of the Club's claim for compensation for the loss of the corner arbour. The Committee considered this amount too little. On 30 January 1931 Findlay had written to St Leger:

> I am really very angry about the way we have been treated in regard to the arbours. I think it is most unfair. Anyway I thank you for saying that you will impress upon Holloways that the work is being undertaken solely at their own risk. I hope the risk is not a serious one, but one never knows, and the position must be made clear to them.

Robertson was instructed to do the best he could, and to tell the authorities that the committee considered that the Club was being treated unfairly, since there was no practical link between the licence for the rebuilding of the arbours and the land required for the splay.

The unveiling of the bas relief.

In the meantime Holloway Brothers had been pressing on with the Wellington Place and St John's Wood Road arbours, and in April presented an architect's certificate for £1,300, being the first instalment of the cost. Payment was deferred for two weeks until the written permission for the work was received from the LCC. Six months later St Leger wrote to say that the balance due to Holloways was £1,849 15s 8d, and that he would be issuing a certificate. MCC's response was that as it was still negotiating with the LCC 'it would be inadvisable at present to pay for the

LORD'S CRICKET GR

arbours in full, but that it would be prepared to meet a certificate of £1,500'.

As the grant of the land was a precondition of formal consent for the new arbours, which had already been built on the strength of the oral permission, the Club had no bargaining power, and Robertson, unsurprisingly, achieved no improvement in the terms that had been offered by the Council.

The splaying of the corner of St John's Wood and Wellington Roads was carried out during the winter of 1931 but, curiously, the surrender of the triangle of land to the Council was not mentioned at the Annual Meeting in May 1932. Nor was any comment included in the Annual Report for 1933. However, at the 1934 Annual Meeting the Committee recorded the matter, putting itself and the Club in the best possible light:

> Representations having been made by the Local Authorities as to the danger to traffic occasioned by the blind corner at the junction of St John's Wood Road and Wellington Road, the Committee have agreed to a few feet of the Club's leasehold property being cut off at this corner and dedicated to the public. By the generosity of Mr David Isaacs a panel in bas relief executed by Mr Gilbert Bayes, the sculptor, depicting 'Athletics', is being placed on the angle wall.

At its meeting on 8 January 1934 the Committee had authorised the Arts and Decorations Sub-Committee to approve the artist's design for the proposed relief in Portland Stone 'unless the Earl of Crawford and Balcarres, Chairman of the Sub-Committee, should take serious objection to it'. The panel was unveiled by the Mayor of Marylebone on 17 July 1934, and it is interesting to note that it is dedicated not to the Club, nor to sport, but to St Marylebone.

Left: The bas relief in its new position, after refurbishment in 1995.

In 1995, as part of a scheme to provide views into the ground to relieve the rather forbidding brick perimeter, the angle wall was demolished. It was replaced by the bas relief between iron railings, the whole set on a plinth of Portland stone. This new screen was set back slightly and floodlighting in the widened pavement illuminates the panel and its call to 'play up, and play the game'.

The Annual Report presented in 1932 recorded that 'the new arbours along the walls of St John's Wood Road and Wellington Place have given every satisfaction. Permission to rebuild permanent arbours along the wall of Wellington Road has not yet been obtained.' This remained the case until 11 January 1937, when the Secretary reported to the Committee that the London & North Eastern Railway had at last given consent for the building of arbours on the east side of the Practice Ground, on the same conditions as had applied in 1931. Designs and estimates had been obtained from three companies, the lowest from the firm of David Rowell, and this was accepted, subject to consent being given by the LCC without unreasonable conditions.

Negotiations for the permission took so long that the building work could not be done before the start of the season, but was deferred until the autumn. By then the contractors had to be granted an increase of £90 over their original tender of £1,909 5s because of a rise in the price of steel. At the AGM on 4 May 1938 the total cost was given as £4,000, and one of the reasons for welcoming the new arbours was that they would provide extra facilities during the Easter cricket classes. Another was that, since the rear walls were set sixty feet in from the wall along Wellington Road, extra car-parking space had become available.

The saga of the arbours had lasted just over eight years.

8

The Lord Harris Memorial

1932–33

George Robert Canning, the fourth Lord Harris, died on 24 March 1932, six weeks after his 81st birthday. For all his life he had been involved with cricket. Born in Trinidad, where his father, the third Baron, was Governor, he had played for Eton, for Oxford, where he was a blue four years running (1871–74), and for Kent. In 1875, on coming down from Oxford he assumed the captaincy of 'his' county and became a member of the Committee of MCC. He inspired a revival of cricket in the county, and of the Band of Brothers, founded originally in 1857, the amateur side that had done much for cricket in Kent, and to which Herbert Baker was elected before he went to South Africa in 1892.

Not a modest man, Harris assumed a leader's role throughout his life. He regarded himself as a true gentleman and prided himself on his honesty and fair-mindedness. But he was unbending, and resisted change with increasing fervour as he grew older. Both in Kent and at Lord's he would not tolerate any breach of the laws of cricket. 'Rules,' he said, 'are made to be broken, laws are made to be kept'. In 1885 he refused to play a return match with Lancashire because two of its bowlers threw

Lord Harris, President 1895,
Treasurer 1916 until his death in 1932.

the ball, and he dismissed from the Kent side two fast bowlers with suspect actions.

An early incident demonstrates both how imperious and how courageous he could be. He went with R. A. Fitzgerald's team to Canada in 1871–72, as did W G Grace, and then in 1878–79 led a team to Australia, at the invitation of the Melbourne Cricket Club. The main match, on the Melbourne ground, is now regarded as the third Test match, and England were well beaten. Harris had hired an umpire for the match and, pleased with his performance, unwisely took him across the state boundary to Sydney for the next game against New South Wales. On the second day, a Saturday, after the second of two blatantly partial decisions, one, on the Friday, giving Harris not out and the other giving the NSW leading batsman run out, the NSW captain, David Gregory, asked Harris, at the pavilion gate, to change the umpire. Harris refused, and with a crowd of protesting spectators gathering around the official, went to the wicket in his defence. One of the crowd, aiming at the umpire, struck Harris with a stick. Still Harris refused to change the umpire, and play had to be abandoned for the day. The match was finished on the Monday, and England won. Although Harris accepted the apology of the NSW Cricket Association, it was, he said 'an occurrence it was impossible he could forget'.

In 1890 he became Governor of Bombay, and immediately on his return, in 1895, President of MCC. In 1901, at the age of fifty, he went to the Boer War with the Imperial Yeomanry as Assistant Adjutant General. In 1916 he succeeded the Rt. Hon. Sir Spencer Ponsonby-Fane as Honorary Treasurer of MCC. Sir Spencer had been elected a member in 1840, Honorary Treasurer in 1880 and a Trustee in 1901. When he died in 1915, he had been a member for seventy-five years and Honorary Treasurer for thirty-five. Harris held that office for a mere sixteen years.

It is difficult to appreciate, at this distance in time and in such different political and social circumstances, the influence that Harris wielded, the control that he exerted over the management of the game, in matters great and trivial alike. Yet in spite of his patriarchal stance, he seems to have been genuinely well-regarded and liked by his fellow committee members. When he celebrated his 80th birthday in February 1931, he was presented by the Club with a Georgian tankard 'in appreciation and admiration of one who as Treasurer of the Club, and in many other ways, has rendered inestimable service to MCC and cricket generally'.

When news of what proved to be his final illness was reported to the Committee on 1 February 1932, the Secretary was instructed 'to convey to him the earnest wishes of the Committee for his early recovery, and to say that all will be thinking of him on the 81st anniversary of his birthday on 3 February'. The first part of the message was a politeness to be expected; the second could spring only from deep respect and perhaps even affection.

The good wishes were of no avail, and on 11 April 1932 the Committee unanimously passed a resolution on the proposition of the President expressing great regret at the loss sustained in the death of the Treasurer. A similar resolution was passed at the AGM on 4 May. The minutes of both meetings record, movingly, that the resolution was passed 'standing'. The records do not note that this courtesy was extended to anyone else in the inter-war years.

Lord Hawke, President during the years of the Great War, and a member of the Committee continuously from 1907 until he retired as Honorary Treasurer at the AGM in 1938, said that Harris was the greatest cricket administrator the game had ever known, and that his name would always be associated with its history. He had done much to keep alive the honourable traditions of the game, and the

Club had the proud right to regard him as its own. At the AGM in 1932, the President (Viscount Bridgeman) said that it was impossible to overstate the services which Lord Harris had rendered to MCC and to cricket, and he hoped that his splendid example would be remembered and followed. The passage of years has done nothing to diminish these assessments of his position. His biographer in *Barclays World of Cricket* says:

> It is arguable that Lord Harris is the greatest figure in cricket history except 'W. G.' No man exercised so strong an influence on the cricket world so long or so wisely, and it is unlikely that, in more democratic days, any man will do so again. He was scrupulously just, a formidable and feared figure, respected, and by those who knew him well and by the many whom he had helped in some difficulty or crisis, deeply loved.

In November 1932 it was decided that he should have a permanent memorial at Lord's, and a special sub-committee of five was appointed. Sir Herbert Baker was asked for proposals, and on 15 December suggested two possibilities. The first demonstrated his tenacity and extreme reluctance, in spite of continued rebuffs, to let go of an idea of which he thought highly. On the excuse that it had been liked by Harris, he resurrected his first suggestion of 1919 for the W. G. Grace Memorial – but on a smaller scale, which would have allowed access for machinery – whereby a 'wall of honour' would be built at the far end of the Match Ground, opposite the Pavilion and between the cantilever stands, with bas relief portraits of great players or engraved inscriptions. Baker's second idea was for a wall at the rear of the lawn on the site of the former open tennis court between the Grace Gates and the Pavilion.

On 6 January 1933 Baker wrote a long letter to MCC enlarging on his original ideas and adding as another suggestion a gateway, similar to the Grace Gates, at the middle entrance in St John's Wood Road, but warning, 'It is not a very pleasant entrance, being near lavatories and the hotel – though it might be made pleasanter if ever the hotel were rebuilt.'

The Sub-Committee favoured the idea of a wall behind the lawn, subject to a suitable entrance being designed. It suggested that some new office accommodation might be incorporated. It was decided that the Club should bear the entire cost of the memorial and not ask for subscriptions, as it had for the Grace Memorial.

On 6 March Baker sent Findlay two drawings illustrating a fine wrought-iron gateway into a cloistered garden, with covered galleries on the north and south sides and an open wall on the west (rear) wall opposite the gate. Baker proposed to use flint for the wall, as it was 'imperishable and appropriate to the chalk hills of Belmont' (Harris's home in Kent). The flint facing was to be framed by two string courses and inset piers of Roach stone, under four courses of tiles and a round ridge-tile.

The idea of incorporating offices had the predictable result that initial costings of £13,700 caused alarm. A modification of Baker's original scheme was proposed, with only the wall on the western side of the lawn. A bronze bust of Harris would be placed centrally, and there would be a broad border of flowers along the wall. This, it was considered, would cost between £600 and £1,000. An alternative, more expensive at £4,000 to £5,000, would be to add a loggia on the south side, with a gateway in, and railings on the east wall which would separate the garden from the carriage drive.

The decision to create a memorial formed part of the annual report for the 1933 AGM. Also reported was the provision of a corrugated asbestos roof over a part of the Mound Stand at a cost of £2,250, which 'it was thought would be more satisfactory than

the old canvas covering on a showery day'. A member was thanked for his help 'in ridding the ground of weeds'. How he achieved this is not recorded.

On 21 June Findlay wrote to Baker. The Committee wanted a modified scheme, with no north or south gallery, but with offices. Baker responded appropriately and found a site for additional offices in the Pavilion, by converting lavatories at the southern end. His revised scheme retained the flint-faced west wall as the main part of the memorial, with the bust opposite a gateway in a new, low front wall, with iron newels and chains, and he reduced the scale of his iron gates. On 1 August Findlay wrote to Baker to say that his drawings had been seen by the Committee the day before and 'if you are satisfied that the modified scheme will look beautiful, please obtain estimates. In no circumstances is the Committee prepared to expend more than £2,000 inclusive of all fees'. Horder & Wells, the quantity surveyors, priced the scheme at £1,702 5s 0d, adding £30 if stone slates rather than tiles were used for the coping above the flint. A further revision of the design was prepared by Baker during October, omitting the arch over the gateway and reducing the height of the piers in the front wall. The design was approved at last on 6 November, and Holloway Brothers' estimate of £1,700 was accepted 'as a firm tender'. Harris's son responded warmly to the idea that the flint should come from the family estate, and allowed Holloways to use the stone from a derelict cottage. At the builders' suggestion, a damp-proof course was introduced between the brick foundation courses and the stone. This is still visible at the southern end of the wall, but for most of the wall's length its effect is negated by the fact that it is several inches below the earth of the rose-bed.

The estimate excluded the cost of any paving. In February 1934 Baker submitted plans for a York stone path leading from the new gateway to the memorial tablet, with a continuation in front of the flower-bed along the entire length of the wall. This was estimated at £285. In March it was decided to re-turf the lawn in front of the memorial, and to erect teak trellis-work between the lawn and the refreshment servery, as the view 'was not in keeping with the memorial'. The trellis was a cheaper solution than Baker's cloister to the problem of separating the lawn from the luncheon tents that then stood to the left of the Grace Gates. What Baker and the Committee of 1934 would have thought of the intrusion into the Memorial Garden of the concrete escape-stairs from the present banqueting suite is not difficult to imagine!

It was decided that an inscribed tablet should be placed on the wall, rather than creating a niche in which a bust could be placed, and the President, with assistance from Viscount Lewisham, Sir Lancelot Sanderson and Sir Kynaston Studd, drafted the inscription:

ERECTED TO THE MEMORY OF
GEORGE ROBERT CANNING
1851 LORD HARRIS 1932
BY THE MCC
IN RECOGNITION OF INVALUABLE SERVICES
RENDERED TO CRICKET AND TO THE CLUB OVER
A PERIOD OF MORE THAN FIFTY YEARS HE WAS
A GREAT CRICKETER A GREAT GENTLEMAN
AND A WISE COUNSELLOR WHOSE
ENTHUSIASM FOR THE GAME NEVER WANED

When the memorial was unveiled on 2 May 1934, the day of the AGM, cricket was suspended for thirty minutes to allow players and staff at Lord's to attend the ceremony, at which the President, Lord Hailsham, gave a rousing speech:

Memorial tablet to Lord Harris.

Members enjoying the peace of the garden seen through the gates.

We are assembled here this afternoon for the purpose of doing honour to one of the greatest figures in the world of cricket in the last half century. If W. G. Grace was the outstanding figure in the cricket world as a player, the late Lord Harris was surely its greatest personality on its administrative side, and it is neat and fitting that the memory of these two great cricketers should be perpetuated at Lord's, which has been described as the Valhalla of the game . . .

Lord Harris placed his great gifts and knowledge ungrudgingly at the disposal of the game which he played and loved so well. His services to the MCC cannot be over-estimated . . . During his long association with the club he did more than any other man to raise it to the unchallenged position which it now holds in the world of cricket. His counsel was always there to lead and guide, and, when need arose to encourage or to restrain.

But great administrative ability rarely issues in full achievement unless it is allied to vision and to ideals. These Lord Harris

possessed in liberal measure. His aim was ever to maintain the greatness of the game to which he devoted such a large part of a singularly full life; to keep its tradition unsullied; and to protect it against the eruption of any tendency likely to conflict with its true spirit.

I make no apology for quoting again the words which he wrote on his eightieth birthday. Appealing to the youth of the country to play as much cricket as they could, this is what he said: 'You do well to love it, for it is more free from anything sordid, anything dishonourable than any game in the world. To play it keenly, honourably, generously, self sacrificingly, is a moral lesson in itself, and the classroom is God's air and sunshine'.

We have with us members of the MCC, and the Surrey team, and I have just received the following telegram from Mr Chapman: 'The Kent team playing at Cardiff today would much appreciate being associated with the unveiling of the Lord Harris Memorial at Lord's, at the same time appreciating his great work for English and Kent cricket'.

We also have present today Sir Herbert Baker and Mr St Leger to whose artistic skill and patience we owe the beautiful and dignified design which I am about to unveil. It is appropriate that it should have been constructed of flint from his Kentish home. It is well that in this place which he served so faithfully and where he spent so many happy hours we should erect a memorial which will

Protect his memory and preserve his story,
Remain a lasting monument of his glory.

This memorial it is now my proud privilege to unveil.

9

Q Stand and After

1933–39

When Sir Herbert Baker came to Lord's in 1919, Block D was immediately to the south of the Pavilion: a small stand with a few rows of its higher seats under cover. In 1924, when the stands were renamed in alphabetical order from the north side of the Pavilion around the ground, this little stand was last in turn, and became 'Q'.

Behind it stood the clock tower, to the right as one entered through the Grace Gates, and beyond the tower were the members' dining room, its extension, and the hotel. The dining room and the hotel had their back walls on the St John's Wood Road boundary, while the dining room extension curved from the room to join the clock tower. The buildings looked towards the Match Ground over the open concourse now occupied by the Tavern Stand.

In July 1933 the Clerk of Works, F. M. Cotterell, prepared a rough plan showing the possibility of increasing the Pavilion accommodation by creating an entrance directly from the first

D Stand (later designated Q Stand) to the south of the Pavilion and in front of the Clock Tower and Members' Dining Room.

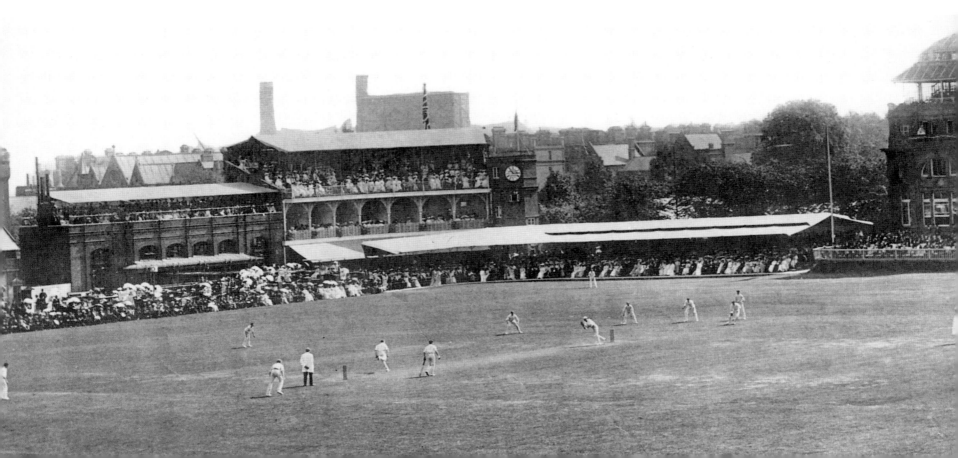

floor into a new stand over the existing seats of Block Q. The upper deck would accommodate 350 members, and it was suggested that the lower terrace could be reconstructed for use by members' friends. The Clerk of Works estimated that the cost would not exceed £6,000.

Baker prepared plans which showed an estimate of £13,500. Not surprisingly, in view of the original figure, he was told to see how much could be saved 'by following the straight line of the existing buildings'.

He then prepared a scheme for a straight stand, and had more precise estimates prepared by Horder & Wells for various alternatives. Leaving the existing stand undisturbed, and adding a straight upper gallery was costed at £5,400, as opposed to a curved upper gallery at £6,475. Removal of the existing stand and the construction of curved lower and upper tiers, with a roof, was priced at £9,200. The bridge to connect the gallery with the Pavilion, including changes to the layout of the rooms at the southern end of the first floor, would add £575.

The estimates and a model were shown to the Sub-Committee, and Baker was asked to reconsider the reconstruction of the lower stand. In a letter to the Secretary on 6 November 1933 he explained that the Club could either cut through the existing stand to build foundations for the new upper stand, then level up the lower stand, which was built on hardcore, or remove the lower stand altogether and form a new one carried by piers and walls to give cellarage accommodation beneath.

His report was presented to the Committee, but no decision was recorded. The payment of architect's fees for the drawings was authorised, on account of any further money that would become due if one of the schemes was adopted. This happened in February 1934, when Baker, Horder & Wells, and Faber were paid

£224. Of this, £111 was to be merged in future fees should work proceed 'substantially on the lines of the existing designs'.

Also on 6 November the Committee considered the question of installing a passenger lift in the Pavilion, and decided that the sites suggested were unsuitable. (This possibility was raised regularly at succeeding AGMs and always met with the same answer, until 1996 when a lift was installed easily and without fuss to one side of the main entrance.)

At the same meeting in November 1933 a letter from Viscount Bridgeman was read, urging an increase in the membership to relieve the congested waiting list. From then on the proposed new stand and possible increases in membership seem to have become linked. The Secretary reported that of the 681 candidates on the list in 1900, only ninety had become ordinary members, forty had not replied to letters, seventy-eight were dead, sixty-eight had been elected as cricketers, fifteen had become life members, and thirteen had withdrawn. He was asked to do more research. Letters were sent to the 3,066 candidates entered in the books between 1901 and 1905 inclusive: 2,276 could not be traced or had died, 614 wished to remain on the list and 176 did not. In all, there were over 12,000 names on the waiting list, and 5,684 members. The limit on membership was 6,000.

Baker did more work on the option for a new, curved lower stand, cellars, and a curved upper gallery in four bays, with a bar and lavatory accommodation. Horder & Wells brought up to date their estimate of cost to £9,650. On 22 March 1934 Baker wrote to tell Faber:

A letter has come from Mr Findlay saying that the Committee propose to recommend that the new stand should be built, but they are seriously worried about the use of reinforced concrete.

You visited Lord's recently in connection with a complaint of this nature. Will you make it convenient to visit Mr Findlay and go into the matter of which he speaks, and also consider this wider aspect of deterioration of reinforced concrete work.

Faber must have been persuasive, because at the AGM in May the Committee continued with its decision to propose that the ceiling on membership should be raised from 6,000 to 7,000 and that authority be given to elect 800 new members in 1935, over and above the 200 annual limit, and subsequently up to 300 additional members a year.

It was recognised that, if this proposal was accepted, the accommodation within the Pavilion would have to be increased. The Annual Report set out the plan to build a new stand over Block Q, with an entrance from the south end of the Pavilion. Block Q would be rebuilt, and, with the new stand, so designed that it could form part of a much larger scheme, including the reconstruction of the buildings between the W. G. Grace Memorial Gateway and the Mound Stand, should the Club at any future date consider it necessary to improve the accommodation on this part of the ground.

The report quoted the cost of the work at between £10,000 and £12,000 and said that it would result in the provision of about 350 extra Pavilion seats, and some 500 more seats in Block Q. The reference to the design presaging a larger scheme was far-sighted. By adopting Baker's design for a curved stand, space was left to the rear for a roadway between the stand and the clock tower.

Baker was instructed to obtain tenders for the new stand and the rebuilding of Block Q, on the condition that the work should begin on 3 September 1934 and be completed by the end of February 1935. Early in June he wrote to Faber with the good news, and confirmed that they were to share equally a fee of eight per cent of the cost of the work.

On 26 June 1934 tenders were returned by seven companies stating prices and contract times. Higgs & Hill quoted £7,372 and twenty-eight weeks, while Holloway Brothers gave £7,900 against a period of twenty-one weeks. More expensive were Mowlam at £8,351 and twenty-four weeks and Trollope & Colls at £8,502 and twenty weeks respectively. Pitcher Construction estimated £8,506 and twenty-four weeks, Bierrum & Partners £9,025 and eighteen weeks and, most expensively, Peter Lind proposed £9,270 and twenty-two weeks.

That afternoon, Faber wrote to Baker to warn him that a severe winter might delay work by up to eight weeks. He pointed out that the twenty-one-week period quoted by Holloways would mean that they had an excellent chance of finishing the reinforced concrete part of the work before very cold weather set in. On 1 August Baker replied that he had been instructed by the Secretary to accept Holloways' tender on account of the favourable time element, which should mean that they finished the 'intricate concrete work' before severe frosts could be anticipated. On the same day Baker told Holloways that their tender had been accepted – not as the lowest in cost, but on the matter of time:

This factor was regarded as the all important one since it is essential to the quality of the concrete that it should be done in good weather conditions and temperature, and it would appear . . . that the more delicate and dangerous work should be completed by Christmas.

On 21 September 1934 the London County Council gave its approval, subject to a number of conditions relating to the foundations, the width of gangways, the quality of steel, and the submission of weekly test-sheets of compressive stress in the concrete. Its final requirement was that the structure must be removed after 1 January 1939 unless the Council had previously consented to its retention for a further period. In a letter dated 25 September Baker reminded the Secretary that this last condition conformed to the restrictions laid down for the other stands, which were all still regarded as temporary structures – presumably so that their condition could be kept under regular review by the authority.

Members of the Committee clearly had lingering concerns about the quality and performance of the reinforced concrete. On 5 October Baker wrote to Faber to say that the appointment of an inspector to oversee the work had been agreed by the Club, and that he would start work on Monday next at £7 7s a week. Holloways had sub-contracted the specialist concrete work to the Leighton Buzzard Concrete Company (1933) Ltd. On 19 October the company wrote to Holloways to confirm that 'we make a practice of setting out the entasis of columns by a curve known as the conchoid of Nicomedes'. This device corrected the visual illusion of the columns appearing concave when erected.

The concrete work was finished at the beginning of February 1935, and all scaffolding and other obstructions around the perimeter of the building were cleared away by the end of that month. Additional expenditure of £220 was approved for painting the whole of the concrete work on the stands, and a further £60 to alter the position of the Pavilion steps in order to widen the passageway between the Pavilion and Q Stand.

At that moment a domestic crisis precipitated a special meeting of the Committee: the Match Ground had been attacked by a plague of leatherjackets, and was in a serious state. The Secretary had sought advice from several authorities on turf, and where possible an exterminator was being applied, but the boggy state of the ground rendered it impossible to make much headway, with the grubs merely coming to the surface and not being killed. Staff were trying to collect the grubs, but in the process were doing damage to the turf.

The Board of Greenkeeping Research, which had inspected the ground, reported that its members knew of no preparation which would kill the grubs. Mr R. H. Twinning was advised that lead arsonate had been applied, with satisfactory results, on the Rye golf course, and that this preparation actually killed the grubs without harming the turf. The Secretary was instructed to make further enquiries, but these do not seem to have led to much success, because the Annual Report prepared for the AGM in May referred to the continuing destruction of the grass roots in various places. Every effort, it was said, was being made to exterminate the grubs.

The same report drew attention to the completion of the new Block Q. The upper gallery, which was regarded as an extension of the Pavilion, and therefore reserved for members, had 350 seats. At ground level the stand extended both in front of the upper gallery and on the south east side, thus providing slightly more seats, with the majority under the cover. (In recent years part of this area has been enclosed to form the Middlesex Club room.)

On 21 June 1935 Alex Scott wrote a note to St Leger to say that the Secretary had telephoned that morning

in a bad state about the temporary end of the new stand at present covered with asbestos sheeting. It appears that the mastic in the joints melts in the sunshine and drips on to the people in the stand. The Test Match is next week and there is dreadful fear that the ladies' dresses will suffer and [this] may lead to trouble.

The back of Q Stand seen from the Pavilion access road.

Findlay insisted that Holloways attend at once to deal with the problem and to ensure absolute protection against any recurrence.

In 1989 Q Stand was renamed the Allen Stand, in honour of Sir George Allen, generally known as 'Gubby', who had been President in 1963 and Honorary Treasurer from 1964 to 1974. A former fast bowler and captain of England, he had given service to cricket matched only by that of Lord Harris. Gubby lived in the house in Grove End Road which, after his death, was acquired by the Club as a home for the Secretary. Ten years later, in 1999, Baker's simple mono-pitch roof was replaced with a structure to a design by David Morley, to accommodate an electronic scoreboard.

Although no doubt disappointed at not being involved in the construction of the third terrace of arbours, on the east side of the Practice Ground, Baker and Scott were busy at Lord's in 1937 and 1938. Baker was 76 in 1938, and although he never really retired, but continued in regular touch with his office and his clients until his death in 1946, his partner had since the mid-1930s begun to assume more and more responsibility.

As war approached, both were developing fascinating and far-sighted plans for MCC. Town-planning control was then in its infancy; nevertheless, its possible impact on Lord's preoccupied the Club from 1933 until the war began.

The Town and Country Planning Act 1932 allowed for the first time schemes to cover already built-up areas, and land not likely to be developed at all. The owner of land injuriously affected by the inception of a scheme could claim compensation from the responsible local authority. Conversely, the local authority could claim three-quarters of the increase in value of land which benefited from a development.

The London County Council announced its intention of preparing a town-planning scheme for most of London, including Lord's Ground. Having interviewed the valuer to the LCC, the Secretary reported to the Committee at its meeting on 29 May 1933 that the ground was to be designated as a private open space. A special Sub-Committee was established to handle the matter. Its members were the President (Viscount Hailsham), the Treasurer (Lord Hawke), Viscount Lewisham, Sir Lancelot Sanderson and Captain the Hon. W. S. Cornwallis. Over the next six years, until the outbreak of war, the LCC and its valuer proved remarkably obdurate in the face of the broadsides fired by this formidable group. After his year as President, Hailsham continued as Chairman, undeterred by any thoughts of conflicts of interest, although he was throughout this time Lord Chancellor, and meetings of the Sub-Committee took place in his room in the House of Lords.

The Committee's initial stance was that the whole of the Club's property, not merely the cricket ground, should be excluded from the proposed scheme. In return, the Club was prepared to give an undertaking to maintain the Match Ground and Practice Ground as a private open space for twenty-five years. It was felt that this line would secure the best interests of the Club, having regard to the tremendous increase in residential land values in St John's Wood.

The Committee maintained this position through 1934 and 1935, without progress, and on 23 July 1935 Sir Lancelot Sanderson, Mr Ringland (the Club's agent) and Colonel Rait Kerr, the Secretary, met Sir Kingsley Wood, Minister of Health, in his room at the House of Commons. (In those days, the Ministry of Health was responsible for Town Planning.) Sir Lancelot said that the Club could not possibly agree to the use of the ground being limited to an open space in perpetuity. The Minister stated that he wished to do everything possible to help MCC, but that the Club's

A post-war view of Q Stand seen from the Tavern Concourse.

property was already included in the Town Planning Scheme, though this scheme had not yet received his final approval. He could not see his way to excluding Lord's from the proposals, and anyway could not understand what objection MCC had to Lord's coming into the scheme, as it was not the intention of the LCC to interfere with the ground in any way while the Club retained it for its present use. Moreover, the Club would benefit, in that care would be exercised as to the type of building allowed in the neighbourhood of the ground.

Sir Lancelot said that for his part he could not understand what benefit would derive to the neighbourhood or to the ratepayers from the inclusion of Lord's in the scheme, since something in the order of £400,000 might become payable by the LCC as compensation if both the Match Ground and the Practice Ground were included. This would be the difference between the value of the ground as potential building land and its value as private open space. The Club wanted no restriction on its freedom to deal with its property as it thought fit, whether that was to transfer the hotel or the bakery to a different part of the ground, or to build new stands, or to engage in development on the residential areas which it owned. MCC desired to be its own master and to be excluded from the scheme.

The result of the meeting was an impasse, with the Minister rather weakly concluding by saying that the matter should be thrashed out with the LCC. This proved impossible, as both sides held their positions, but the Club was anxious to know where it stood because extensive redevelopment was under discussion. The completion of Q Stand should have been the first step in a major project for refashioning the south-western corner of the ground.

In May 1937 Baker and Scott met the Secretary and the Assistant Secretary (Ronald Aird) at Lord's to discuss the rebuilding of the hotel on the corner of St John's Wood Road and Grove End Road on part of the land that had originally been 2 Grove End Road. A new hotel would provide bars and a public restaurant on the ground floor, a members' restaurant on the first floor and either two or four staff flats on the second floor. Also at ground level, behind the public restaurant, would be the kitchen serving both the public and the members, and behind the kitchens two rooms facing the garden, for the use of members. Colonel Rait Kerr enlarged on this idea in a letter to Baker of 28 May 1937 in which he said that the members' rooms could act as 'a reading room to attract the best class of person during the winter period'.

The removal of the old hotel would allow the members' luncheon room and its extension, together with the shop and off-licence, to be rebuilt in enlarged form, with ten boxes on the roof. The shops would open onto the road, as well as onto the ground, and there would be a new bakery, the need for which seemed to be constantly on the minds of Committee members. On 19 July 1937 Baker sent plans, sections and elevations of his proposal. Horder & Wells estimated the cost at between £30,000 and £32,000. A few days later Scott sent plans for the new hotel.

If the Committee had gone ahead with the plans, the corner site would not have been lost to the Club through the development of the Century Court flats; the present Tavern – widely considered an architectural disaster – would probably never have come into being; and the debate about the provision of hotel accommodation on the ground, which continues to this day, would not carry with it the threat of further incursion into the Practice Ground. However, Baker and Scott conceived an alternative, more ambitious plan for the corner site which appealed to the Sub-Committee more than the Rait Kerr proposal, and the hotel remained where it was until 1966.

The new scheme took advantage of the notation in the draft town-planning scheme for commercial use of the corner site. Baker and Scott sketched shops and a bakery on the corner, with flats above. When, however, a formal application for planning permission was made, it was refused because the Council decided that shops would be inappropriate in such a predominately residential area. Furthermore it was felt that the plans showed excessive site-coverage. On 11 March 1938 Rait Kerr wrote to Baker to agree that the grounds of refusal were unsatisfactory, and he promised that the Committee would consider the position.

MCC appears to have accepted the Council's revised notation of the corner for residential use, and the architects went back to the drawing-board. Instead of renewing the hotel option, they now suggested a block of flats on ground and two upper floor-levels, built of brick under a pitched, tiled, roof. These were being discussed with the planners when the international situation made further progress impossible.

At the same time as the future of the south-western corner of the ground was being considered, the need for extra office space was becoming urgent. The Secretary had for some time been warning the Committee that he had a growing work-load, and needed additional room for secretarial and clerical staff. In October 1936 he asked, and the Committee agreed, that Baker and Scott should explore the possibility of creating office space by building a floor in the upper part of the large arch at the rear of the Pavilion. The plans showed that this could be done, while retaining at least eleven feet of headroom beneath the arch.

By then Victor Helbing seems to have taken over MCC work from St Leger in Baker's office: it was he who made the application to the LCC in December 1936, stressing urgency, as the Club wanted the work completed by 1 April 1937. Consent was received from the Council in January, and the Club authorised the work, provided it did not cost more than £900. On 2 February Ashby & Horner provided an estimate of £890, but said that the work would take ten weeks – so a decision was made to defer the start until September. The builders agreed to hold their price, but their final account was for £946 14s 8d. Baker's fee (shared with Faber) was an additional eight per cent.

By 1939 the East Gate lavatories had fallen into a very dilapidated condition, and they were rebuilt, at a cost of £3,500, in a different position, so that the East Gate turnstiles could be moved to reduce congestion on match days. There is no evidence that Baker and Scott were involved with this mundane improvement, but they had a rather more glamorous job on the opposite side of the ground where the Club provided the Assistant Secretary with a house at 20 Elm Road, once the home of Thomas Hood. By the end of the 1930s it was coming to the end of its life, so Baker and Scott designed a replacement which was completed in August 1938 at a cost of £5,752 3s 3d, exclusive of architects' fees of six per cent. This was the Club's last major construction project before the war began in September 1939.

10

The Second World War

1939–45

The growing awareness of impending war in Europe was reflected early in the minutes of the MCC Committee. At its meeting on 10 October 1938 the Secretary reported that the Practice Ground had been occupied by an Anti-Aircraft Detachment, 'but that no appreciable damage had been suffered'. Permission had been granted, also, to the London Fire Brigade to make use of the ground as a station for the Auxiliary Fire Service

During the winter the touring team went to South Africa, while at home the Committee agreed to take an early surrender of the lease of 6 Elm Tree Road, which was in such bad condition that it needed to be demolished and rebuilt. The cost was estimated at £5,500, which would come from the Rebuilding Fund. By February 1939 the Secretary was receiving requests for the use of the ground in the case of war, and the Committee instructed him to ascertain from the Air Ministry what official view was held on the matter. The reply was that the Balloon Command proposed to locate one barrage balloon at Lord's, and permission was sought for exercises to take place as soon as April. Furthermore, a searchlight detachment could be expected in August. The Committee consented, subject to receiving an indemnity against damage.

In April, while the Club's architect prepared detailed plans for

Men of the Auxiliary Fire Service, training on the Tavern Concourse.

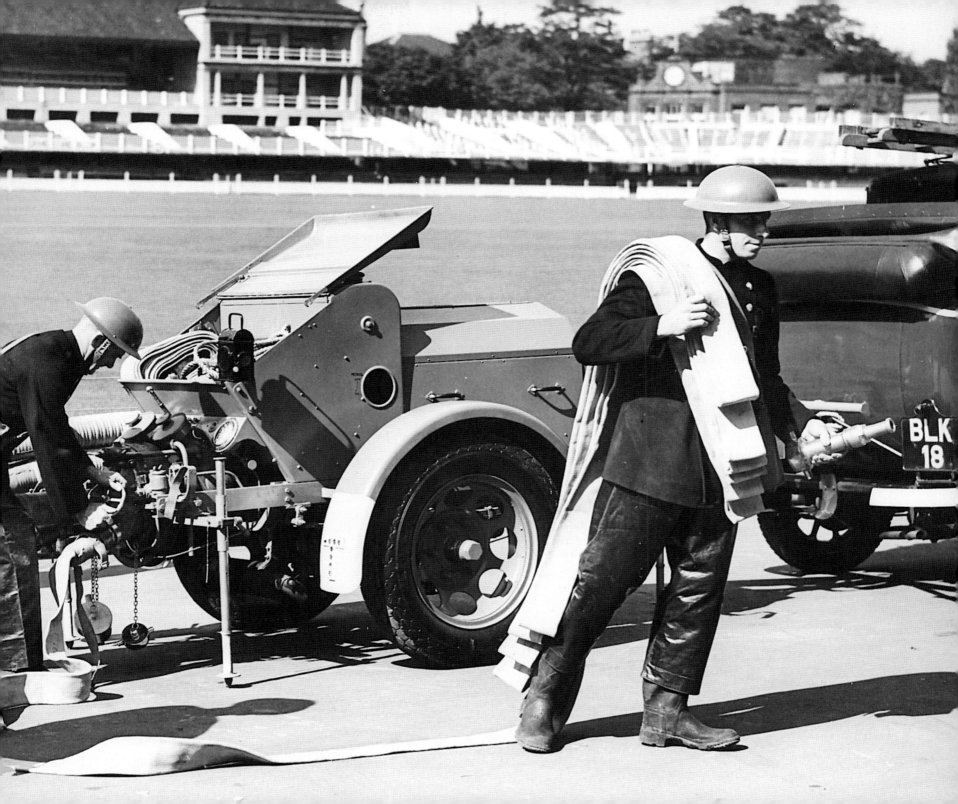

the new house at 6 Elm Tree Road, one of the neighbours sought permission from the Club to erect a bomb-shelter in his garden. The Committee decided to defer plans for the new bakery, partly because of the political uncertainty, and partly because the District Surveyor, although approving the plans, had referred them to the LCC in case that authority had objections from a town-planning point of view. It was proposed to locate the bakery in the disused Racket Court, and its cost would be about £3,500. Members were assured in the Annual Report that although this would mean the loss of one squash court, the two that remained would be adequate for current requirements. Routine matters were attended to, as usual. The West Indies touring team was expected in May, and the toast-list for the dinner to welcome it was settled. An invitation to send a team to India in the coming winter was accepted.

The Committee continued to meet as normal until 24 July 1939, the start of the summer recess. After the declaration of war on 3 September, the Emergency Committee met for the first time on 11 September. The President reported that the Secretary had already left for military service, and that the Assistant Secretary, Aird, would be leaving soon. It was decided to appoint as Secretary William Findlay, Rait Kerr's predecessor from 1926 to 1936, although he could undertake to attend at Lord's only once a week; and also to accept the offer of help from Sir Pelham Warner and appoint him as Assistant Secretary. Warner soon learnt, in his own words, that the secretarial duties are not all about cricket. Lord's was, and is, an estate requiring day-to-day management. Aird reported that all lights had been blacked out, seats removed and Air Raid Shelters provided. The pictures of historical value had been taken down and stored in the basement. The demolition of 6

Elm Tree Road was deferred, as were pending repairs to the cantilever stands.

The barrage-balloon unit and the searchlight detachment were joined by an Auxiliary Fire Service sub-station, and 400 men and thirty officers of the 4th County of London Yeomanry messed in the garden of 2 Grove End Road for a week. By December, tenants of several of the Club's houses were requesting variations in the terms of their leases, either as to rent or the giving of notice.

The Annual Report, presented to the AGM on 1 May 1940, recorded that the paintings which had hung in the Long Room had been moved to safer quarters, as also had the Library, the drawings of distinguished cricketers from the Writing Room and the photographs of past presidents from the Committee Room. Members were told also of the detachments of the forces quartered in different parts of the ground. They had been given facilities for cricket in September and football afterwards, which 'it is satisfactory to be able to record have been greatly appreciated by all ranks'.

Later in May, Oscar Faber wrote to the Club after a joint inspection he had made with the District Surveyor of the cantilever stands. A previous application of asphalt to cover shrinkage cracks had worked loose in places, and other maintenance work was required. Faber had told the District Surveyor that 'the work required a great deal of expert supervision of highly trained men, and that such are engaged on urgent work of the first national importance, from which they cannot be diverted … I am definitely of the opinion that no harm would result if the work were postponed until next summer, or until the war is over, assuming, as I think we safely can, that this will occur before the issue of the next LCC licence, which I believe becomes due in 1943'. The District Surveyor agreed.

The next piece of Club property to be devoted to the war effort

The Nursery Ground in its wartime uniform with the arbours in the background.

was the garage of 4 Grove End Road, which was taken over by the National ARP Animals Committee as an animal first-aid post. Shortly afterwards, the house was occupied by the Home Guard.

In September 1940 the Deputy Secretary had to report to the Emergency Committee the first catalogue of damage from bombing. The roofs of the Pavilion and the Grand Stand had been hit and set on fire by incendiaries, one of which had created a hole in the ceiling of the Long Room. Nos 4, 8 and 14 Grove End Road had also been hit by incendiary bombs, together with a greenhouse in the garden of number 2. The roofs of some of the arbours had been damaged by the cable from a balloon, which had broken away.

On 8 October 1940 a high-explosive bomb fell in the garden of 6 Grove End Road, demolishing part and leaving the rest of the structure unstable. Number 8 was also so seriously damaged as to

Right: The Pavilion secured against bomb blast.

Below: The Committee Room bereft of pictures and with the windows boarded up.

be uninhabitable, while 4, 10, 12, and 14 were less badly affected. None of the tenants was injured. On the same night, 16 Grove End Road was hit by two oil incendiary bombs and rendered unstable. One person died.

A week later an oil incendiary fell in the outfield at the Nursery End of the Match Ground, and Warner reports in his book *Lord's 1787–1945* that when it burst there was found a photograph of a young German officer and written across it, 'With compliments'. Warner records also that Lord's had a narrow escape on 1 November when a high-explosive bomb demolished the synagogue and a corner of the flats opposite the Grace Gates.

At the December meeting Warner reported that an incendiary had caused slight damage to 22 Elm Tree Road, the Secretary's residence, and a 1,000lb high-explosive bomb had fallen on the Match Ground, making a large crater in the north-east corner of the field and breaking the windows of the hotel and of the Committee Room. Furthermore, the cable of the barrage balloon

had caused damage again. This time it had wrapped itself round Father Time and pulled the figure from the roof of the Grand Stand, down on to the seats below.

The Annual Report in May 1941 recorded the considerable damage done to the Club's property and praised the work of the Lord's Fire Fighter Squad, which, with help from the military and fire services, had quickly brought the blazes under control. Apart from the incendiary bombs which had hit premises, it was estimated that between thirty and forty had fallen on the Match and Practice Grounds.

No further bomb-damage was reported after the end of 1940 until the flying bomb attacks began in 1944. Then Lord's had a near miss when a V-1 demolished the wing of a block of flats at the corner of Grove End Road and on the other side of the road broke the windows of the Roman Catholic church. (Built in 1836, this appears in many early prints of the ground.) The final destruction was of 6 Elm Tree Road, which was demolished by an incendiary bomb in March 1945, thus doing what the Club had planned to do in 1940.

In May 1941 Alex Scott was retained by the Club to submit a claim, under the War Damage Act, for compensation for the damage to 16 Grove End Road – which he did in the sum of £352 6s 10d. Scott claimed a fee of £34 11s 1d, and the War Damage Committee allowed £16 15s 6d. A Ministry of Works licence was received in August, to erect a temporary roof and make other necessary repairs . The house was so badly damaged that it was scheduled for demolition, but Scott recognised its quality and appealed against the decision. In this he was successful, and the building was re-classified as badly damaged, but worth repairing.

In the middle of 1941 the RAF requisitioned the Practice Ground and its buildings, and in January 1942 extended its grip to include the Members' Luncheon Room for the use of the NAAFI. The Emergency Committee noted in February that it was proposed to place a machine gun at the end of the Match Ground.

Throughout the war the Air Ministry paid MCC a compensation rent of £2,500 per annum, inclusive of rates, plus £1,500 per annum for services, insurance and wages. Any damage done to the Club property was the subject of a separate claim. A minimum amount of routine maintenance work was done by MCC staff during the next four winters. Cricket was played during the seasons, and the Refreshment Department seems to have remained active under the leadership of the redoubtable Mr Portman, whose salary was increased from 1 January 1943 to £1,000, in addition to which he was granted a bonus of £250 net of tax for 1942, and a gift of £500 in consideration of his having completed forty years' continuous service to MCC.

On 29 September 1944, the Air Ministry finally released most of the Club property it had requisitioned .

11

Picking Up the Threads

1944–53

The first half of 1944 was a busy time for Baker and Scott. At the beginning of the year the Emergency Committee set up a General Purposes Sub-Committee, to which it delegated responsibility for the Club's property and building work. Its chairman was Colonel the Hon. Sir Stanley Jackson. At its first meeting a report from Scott cautioned that Government control over all building work was likely to continue for a considerable time after the cessation of hostilities.

He suggested an order of priority, giving first place to repairs and the restoration of existing buildings before the ground opened for the first post-war cricket season. He then picked up the threads of pre-war discussion and listed the housing schemes for Grove End Road and Elm Tree Road, followed by the linked projects of a new hotel and members' dining rooms on the corner of the two roads, and the building of an extension to Q Stand and a new stand over the site of the existing Hotel.

The Club asked Scott to survey the condition of all the buildings on the ground, and the houses. His report, dated 14 March 1944, records that in the Pavilion the RAF was still occupying rooms on the top floor. On the ground floor one corner of the Long Room ceiling had been seriously damaged by

an incendiary bomb; many of its windows were without glass, and the plaster mouldings were damaged. 'This room,' he wrote with some understatement, 'requires a good clean and redecoration'. The tennis court and the north and east arbours had been damaged by blast. The south arbours and some rooms under the Mound Stand were occupied by the RAF, and the members' dining room by the NAAFI.

Between the wars the Club had looked to the local firm of Anscombe & Ringland for advice on its houses. It was Mr W. Ringland who had brought to the Club's notice in 1929 the opportunity to acquire the block of houses that had completed MCC's ownership of the whole island site. He had been succeeded as senior partner of the firm by Mr C. H. Gorringe, who at the end of February 1944 gave advice as to whether the redevelopment in Grove End Road should be with houses or flats. In consequence of that the Sub-Committee, early in March, recommended that the site of 2 Grove End Road should be left available for future requirements of the Club, and that Baker and Scott should prepare a sketch scheme for flats on the site of 4–10 Grove End Road, leaving the houses 12, 14 and 16 Grove End Road to be restored.

However, Gorringe was approaching retirement, and at its meeting of 28 March the Chairman of the Sub-Committee raised the question of professional advice. He paid tribute to the opinions which had so far been obtained, but stressed that the advice of a surveyor of high standing, if possible with a knowledge of the neighbourhood, should be sought. He considered that Farebrother Ellis & Company, who were acquainted with the district, would be a suitable firm to advise the Club on how to develop the property to show the best return without spoiling the amenities of the ground.

On the same day, Scott had a discussion with the Sub-

The Imperial Cricket Memorial Gallery.

Committee about the future. He was authorised to prepare a sketch scheme for a new building between the hotel and the clock tower to replace the existing luncheon rooms. It would need to contain a shop and public dining room on the ground floor, a members' dining room on the first floor, and a bakery and kitchen on the top floor. The boxes in the Clock Tower were to be converted into a members' luncheon room, and the Tower linked by a bridge to an extended Q Stand. If Scott recalled the instructions given to Baker in 1937 he will have experienced a sense of *déjà vu*.

On 3 May 1944 he submitted sketches of the proposed new building, but completion of the detailed plans was delayed as his offices suffered bomb damage. On 2 August, however, they were ready, and he asked that they should be regarded as part of a larger scheme for the future. The proposed new building covered the land between the hotel and the Grace Gates. Apart from the restaurants for the members and the public, there was on the second floor both the bakery and kitchen, and a stand seating 1,150. The plan was approved in principle.

By then, however, the Sub-Committee was in a quandary. Since giving Scott instructions about the land in Grove End Road, the Club had received its first report and advice from E. Munro Runtz, the senior partner of Farebrother Ellis. He had assumed that, apart from governing cricket, the MCC was responsible for presenting the game at Lord's for the enjoyment of its members, the players, and the public. He went on: 'Bearing in mind how often a business has no scope for development owing to shortage of land . . . your Committee may find it prudent in the future to widen the facilities offered.' He advised that the sites of both 2 and 4 Grove End Road should be retained for possible future extension of the ground. The site of Number 6 was covered materially by the tennis and

racket courts, and he thought that what was left of the site should also be kept in hand. His proposals would have added about one and one-third acres to the ground. They did however conflict with the instructions given earlier to Scott to design flats for the site of 4–10 Grove End Road.

Runtz recommended also that the ends of the gardens of 8, 10 and 12 Grove End Road should be incorporated into the ground (this suggestion was implemented when the Coronation Garden was created). Finally, he said that even if planning consent could be obtained to transfer the hotel to the corner site, he would regard that as a 'cardinal mistake'. He admitted to being a traditionalist, and wanted the hotel to stay where it was, with the concourse in front of it. He expressed the view, quite strongly, that the hotel should be rebuilt, together with its ancillary buildings on the site it then occupied.

Having prevaricated until December, the Sub-Committee recommended that for the time being no further consideration should be given to the major scheme of building a new bakery, kitchen and luncheon rooms. The difficulty of obtaining materials, building licences and labour had combined to make the Sub-Committee accept with relief Mr Runtz's advice that with the introduction of ventilation and air conditioning the existing bakery could be made satisfactory.

When the Air Ministry relinquished its main occupation of the Club's premises from 29 September 1944, MCC submitted a claim for £3,365 10s 6d for damages. But then it received an unpleasant financial jolt. In the middle of 1944 Scott had woken up to the fact that the Club owed his partnership a considerable amount of money for work done in 1937 and 1939, and never billed. On 27 October he rendered an account for nearly £1,200.

The Emergency Committee accepted that it should pay for the

plans for the housing development in Elm Tree Road, the drawing for the new house at 6 Elm Tree Road, and the report on the Grace Gates stonework, together with an abortive fee for the sketch plans for new stands between Q Stand and the Mound Stand and flats for staff on the corner of Grove End Road. But it was not very happy to be charged a fee for the plans for the development of flats along Grove End Road (for which permission had been refused), on the grounds that the architects should not have done so much work before sounding out the views of the Planning Authority.

An office note from Scott to Baker dated 6 February 1945 said: 'I had a long meeting with Sir Stanley Jackson and Sir Pelham Warner and Colonel Henson and explained that it was not our fault that the LCC turned down the scheme for development at the corner, and that the Committee dropped the whole subject instead of taking our advice and seeking a compromise with LCC. Jackson said we should have known LCC's restrictions. I said MCC as lessee of the site ought to have known them, and when we received instructions at various meetings we assumed MCC knew what it could do. This cleared the air.'

Scott was right. His forthright rejoinder carried the day, but at a price. On 19 February 1945 Henson sent a cheque for £408 4s 9d, the balance owing from the original account, saying in a covering letter, 'The Committee has decided to abandon for the present any major project. Would you please confirm that if in the future it proceeded with either of the schemes you prepared in 1944 you would waive your charges.' Scott confirmed that he would – and in less than two weeks Henson wrote back to him to say that the Club now wanted to proceed with plans for alterations and additions to the hotel and the luncheon rooms.

Scott submitted plans for the July meeting of the Sub-Committee, and they were approved. He thought that it might take eighteen months to obtain a building licence, and was asked to provide an approximate estimate of the likely cost of the work, but there is no record that he did so. Attention seems to have been deflected to the staff flats for which a licence was being sought.

In April 1945 Sir Pelham Warner prepared a memorandum on the accommodation of spectators at Lord's after the war. In his preamble he commented that although suggested alterations to the hotel, the bakery and improvements to the members' luncheon room had been reviewed 'again and again,' the accommodation of the general public had not been considered sufficiently. He regarded the seating of spectators as of primary and immediate importance. (At that time Lord's held a maximum of 33,800 spectators. This was the official number returned on the second day, Saturday, 25 June, of the England v Australia match in 1938, when the gates were closed before the start of play. Of the total, some thousands stood or sat on the grass.)

Warner accepted that Lord's could never hope to rival attendances at the four main grounds in Australia, because of restrictions imposed by the Town & Country Planning Act, and the necessity of preserving what he described as the unrivalled atmosphere and charm of Lord's. It would have been more accurate to say that one factor limiting capacity had been the Committee's lack of foresight in failing to accept Runtz's advice to retain for expansion the land with frontage to Grove End Road. Had it done so, it is unlikely that the Planning Authority would have refused consent for the ground to be extended by the incorporation of what remained of the houses.

Warner went on to say that he thought it was within the power of the Club to increase accommodation by some six or seven thousand spectators – something that he believed necessary in view of the fact 'that the aeroplane has brought even such far flung countries as Australia, South Africa and India within a comparatively few hours of England'. He centred his attention on the Grand Stand, a building of which it seems he had become increasingly less fond as time had gone by. It was in this memorandum that he coined his often-quoted comment, 'Never in cricket history has so large a stand held so few spectators'. It was, he said:

> a mass and a maze of staircases, not unlike a Meccano puzzle. The architects indeed seem to have gone 'staircase mad', the lavatories are commodious to a degree and the luncheon rooms at the back of the boxes waste a great deal of space. Further, there are several nooks and corners which look like the sort of dungeon in which The Man in the Iron Mask or Rudolph Rassendyll in *The Prisoner of Zenda* was incarcerated. To anyone who has examined this stand, it is clear that many additional seats could be provided by attacking its underbelly and by doing away with some of the boxes, which are not likely to be in such demand in the future as has been the case in the past. Retain what may be called the main structure, but operate internally.

No record appears to exist of the reception which this memorandum received.

In a letter written to Colonel Henson on 30 May 1945, Runtz included the suggestion that 12 Grove End Road should be used by the Club as a social centre and museum. 'It is not a house,' he wrote, 'that has any artistic merit, but it should lend itself to such a use admirably because of its seclusion and adjacency to the land to be taken from the gardens of numbers 8 and 10 Grove End Road; moreover, the width of the garden being about eighty feet, it should be practicable later on to build a picture gallery about twenty feet wide against the southern boundary without spoiling the amenity of the garden'.

When the recommendations contained in the letter were considered at the meeting of the Sub-Committee on 10 July, no specific reference appears to have been made to this suggestion, giving the impression that the alternative use of number 12 had not been approved. Another opportunity had been lost.

The Club was now beginning to prepare for a return to peacetime arrangements. The Emergency Committee agreed that for the purpose of the resolution at the Special General Meeting of 1940 which had empowered the Emergency Committee, 'the end of the war' should be regarded as the date of the 1946 Annual General Meeting. Two steps towards this return to normality were the merging of the General Purposes and Finance Sub-Committees and the re-establishment of a Property & Works Sub-Committee. The latter convened for the first time in its new form on 26 November 1945, and began its meeting by solemnly considering the accuracy of the minutes of its last meeting on 6 July 1939. Later it was noted that John Markham, FRIBA, had been consulted about the creation of a gallery and library as a War Memorial.

On 5 December 1945, Markham wrote to Alex Scott saying,

> I was asked a week or so ago by Colonel Rait Kerr to advise on fitting out an existing building to house pictures, prints and books as a War Memorial. My name was given to him by a friend who knew of my gallery and library work in the Office of Works. I learn that really you are their regular architect and before proceeding I thought I ought to communicate with you.

I should not be happy to proceed without your knowledge and concurrence.

The next day Scott replied to say that he appreciated this courtesy and would not think of taking any action 'to queer your pitch'. He ended with the possibly ambiguous comment, 'Go ahead and I wish you the best of luck'.

The 'existing building' to which Markham referred was the disused racquets court, and in the annual report presented to members in May 1946 it was stated that the Committee felt that the provision of a gallery and reading room would be a suitable form of memorial to members and imperial cricketers who had given their lives in the war. Markham produced his designs, but by mid-1947 the Secretary had to report that the prospect of obtaining a licence for the work was not promising.

The President (Viscount Cobham) offered to discuss the matter informally with the Minister of Works and the Secretary of State for the Dominions. At the next meeting of the Committee the Secretary reported that Australia would probably present all the timber required for the memorial project. It was minuted that in view of the interest taken in the scheme by the Government, the Secretary should be authorised to apply for a licence for the project. The Committee was over-confident: in October the reply was that after careful consideration at a high level it was not possible to give permission at the present time for the project.

In the first half of 1949 the Secretary made an informal approach to the Ministry of Works to see if there might be a possibility of obtaining a licence to proceed with the scheme on the grounds that it would be a contribution towards the Festival of Britain in 1951. The timing was fortunate, and the application was this time successful. Further good news came in the form of

a decision by the LCC that the conversion of the old racquets court did not constitute development, as defined by the Town and Country Planning Act, and therefore no permission was required and no development charge payable.

The Annual Report of May 1950 recorded that work had begun. Very soon, however, a significant problem became apparent. In August 1949 Markham had submitted rough estimates for the memorial, amounting to £8,000, and a building licence for £8,800 had been obtained from the Ministry. By June 1950, however, it was clear that the estimates were much too low, and the architect had revised his opinion of the minimum cost to £14,600. He was asked to make every effort to reduce the cost as much as possible without materially affecting the dignity of the scheme.

Things went from bad to worse, and by March 1951 it was clear from tenders already received that the cost would be at least £20,000, including interior furnishing. It was agreed that in the light of the serious financial position of the club at that time the idea would have to be abandoned.

It had been the original intention that a library should form part of the memorial. With the decision not to go ahead, at least for the time being, the Committee agreed that the old general office should be furnished with book cases and become the Club's library. By the time of the Annual General Meeting in May 1952, Markham's revised plans for the Imperial Cricket Memorial Gallery had been approved. A tender from Holland Hannen & Cubitts Ltd, amounting to £8,641, was accepted.

The gallery was formally opened by the Duke of Edinburgh on Monday 27 April 1953, before a distinguished gathering which included High Commissioners, great cricketers past and present, and the Australian team, recently arrived for their tour. The memorial was dedicated by the Bishop of London, Dr William

depth of the new building. Finally, in the middle of 1952, it was agreed to take into the curtilage of Lord's the last seventy feet of these rear gardens, in order to create an amenity that all visitors to the ground might use.

The Committee agreed that the details of the layout should be left to the Treasurer, Mr G. C. Newman, and the Deputy Secretary, and the work was carried out in the winter of 1952–53. Inevitably the area became known as the Coronation Garden, and it has proved a popular, shady picnic spot. A feature is the weeping ash planted in memory of the former Secretary and President of the club, William Findlay, who died on 19 June 1953.

Wand, and its intention is made plain on the tablet, which bears a quotation from James Russell Lowell, chosen by the Hon. George Lyttelton:

TO THE MEMORY OF CRICKETERS OF ALL LANDS WHO GAVE
THEIR LIVES IN THE CAUSE OF FREEDOM, 1914–1918: 1939–1945

SECURE FROM CHANGE IN THEIR HIGH HEARTED WAYS

That same year also saw the opening of a new garden for the enjoyment of spectators. When Runtz had first suggested in 1944 that the gardens of 8, 10 and 12 Grove End Road should become part of Lord's, he had recommended appropriating a depth of about forty-six feet. In 1947, when the rebuilding of A enclosure was being considered, it was felt that fifty-eight feet would need to be taken in order to accommodate the extra

Top left: The dedication of the Imperial Cricket Memorial by the Bishop of London following the formal opening of the Gallery by the Duke of Edinburgh on 27 April 1953.

Left: Spectators enjoying their picnics in the Coronation Garden.

12

The Warner Stand

1954–58

In 1954 a membership crisis once again precipitated a major building project, as it had in 1933. The number of candidates proposed annually was now more than four times natural wastage, and the period of waiting before election close to thirty years. As the problem was debated, so too were the plans to replace the old Block A with a modern stand that would give increased accommodation for an enlarged membership and the new category of Associate members.

When Herbert Baker had been asked to advise on the provision of increased stand accommodation in 1923, Block A was already forty years old. Originally three rows of fixed seats had been installed for the public and over the years more rows and a roof had been added. Baker had proposed adding an upper tier to provide 1,000 extra seats at a cost of about £4,000. The Committee rejected the idea, fearing that it would obstruct the view of play for those in carriages behind the stand. This caused Baker to write to the President in astonishment:

> Having regard to the great value of this position, which is one of the best on the field, it would appear a great pity not to take advantage of the scheme for providing more than a thousand

seats which would be occupied during Test and other big popular matches, whereas on the one or two occasions that coaches were made use of those seats could be kept empty by the simple expedient of blocking the staircase.

This logic cut no ice, and Block A remained unaltered. Similarly, and perhaps even more surprisingly, when the provision of more accommodation for members and the public was being considered towards the end of the 1930s, attention focussed on the area around the hotel, rather than in the north west corner of the Ground. The hold that the old stand had over some members was referred to by Diana Rait Kerr in her book *Lord's 1946–70*, when she called it 'the stronghold of the most elite socialites of their day, and until its final closing a much loved haven of the more discerning friends and families of members and players.'

It was not until July 1947 that the Property & Works Sub-Committee suggested reconstructing the stand. It was thought that between 1,500 and 2,000 additional seats could be obtained by building a double-decker stand, the upper level unroofed, and with a space for newsreel and television cameras on the upper level and extra Press facilities. It was recognised that the extra depth of the block would require the incorporation into the ground of part of the rear gardens of 8, 10 and 12 Grove End Road. Most importantly, the project depended on obtaining a licence from the Ministry of Works. This was not forthcoming, and nothing more was done until the summer of 1949, when Alex Scott prepared some sketch plans. The Property & Works Sub-Committee regarded these as being 'not entirely satisfactory' but used them to support an informal approach to the Ministry of Works, repeating the request for a licence.

The Sub-Committee met annually in the years immediately

after the war, but in July 1950 there was no reference to the fate of the 1949 application, and none appeared until July 1954, when the Committee considered a suggestion that Block A should be rebuilt as an extension to the Pavilion. The Chairman, G. C. Newman, said that he had discussed the idea with Louis de Soissons, RA, and had shown him Scott's sketches.

This was the second time that the name of de Soissons had appeared in the Club's records. Earlier in the year the Committee had approved expenditure of £1,100 for the redecoration of the Long Room, and the formation of two built-in show-cases in lieu of the fire places. Louis de Soissons had been retained to advise.

His appointment marks the end of the Baker years, and Scott is not mentioned again in the records. Baker, who had been the Club's architect for twenty-seven years, had died on 4 February 1946, an occasion that passed without comment from the Committee. After Baker's death, Scott had taken Victor Helbing into partnership. Like Baker, Scott never retired.

Kenneth Peacock from de Soissons' firm became the architect for the new stand, and on 25 November 1954 he showed sketch plans to the Property & Works Sub-Committee. The design provided for a minimum of 1,700 additional seats and included two bars for the use of members, and facilities for the Press and BBC. He also produced detailed plans showing what shadows the new stand would cast across the ground. He assured the meeting that, providing British Summer Time was maintained, the shadows would at worst only just reach the north-west corner of the square by 6.30 pm at the end of August.

The estimated cost of the stand, excluding seats, was £58,380, which with fees would rise to around £68,000. Peacock proposed that it be built in two separate stages. The first, which would include the main fabric and be an open steel structure, would be

Left: The skeleton of the Warner Stand rises in 1957.

Right: The Warner Stand under construction.

ready by the spring of 1956, thus enabling some seats to be used for that season, when the Australians were due to tour. The second stage, consisting of all the ancillary work, would be carried out in the following winter so that the stand would be completed by the spring of 1957.

When the Sub-Committee met next, in April 1955, Peacock produced more detailed drawings and a revised estimate of cost, which showed a substantial increase to £85,595, excluding seats and fees. The total cost of the project would therefore have been about £100,000. Anticipating that this news would cause dismay, Peacock had drawn sketch-plans of three new schemes. In each case he had omitted the Press and BBC accommodation, and considerably reduced the facilities for refreshment. A by-product of these revisions was that whereas the original scheme provided for 2,469 seats, the three new proposals had a seating capacity of around 3,000. It was suggested that the additional accommodation for the media could be found in the Bowlers' annexe. To convert this into a Press box would cost around £5,000, and entail providing alternative changing rooms for professionals, for which a tentative figure of £4,000 had been allocated.

Peacock was asked to work up two of the three alternatives and report back to the next meeting of the Sub-Committee in June. At that meeting the design which he produced contained seats for 2,870 spectators on two levels, with toilet accommodation and two separate bars. The media space had been omitted. The estimated cost of the project was £69,790, plus fees and seats, giving a total of £85,843. It was decided to recommend that the Club proceed with this proposal. Peacock was by now uncertain as to the availability of the seats for the 1956 season, because it was unlikely that the steel could be obtained in time. In August 1955 he recommended that a contract should be let for the whole of the

work as from September 1956 and should continue until completion without a break. In this way he felt that the structure and seating could at least be ready for the 1957 season.

There remained some dissent in the Property & Works Sub-Committee. After a long debate at the October meeting it was agreed that Peacock should be asked to submit new plans which reinstated media accommodation on the top tier, but without bars, and with lavatories below ground level. As a measure of economy the stands should not be of cantilever construction. Peacock was clearly unhappy about this, and at the next meeting of the Sub-Committee in December members changed their minds yet again and agreed that cantilever construction should be adopted, since this would increase seating capacity. Some members thought that in view of the omission of a bar, one should be constructed in the Coronation Garden. The Chairman pointed out that this would take up more than a third of the garden, and anyway the Committee had already turned down a previous proposal to have a permanent structure there. Peacock reinstated the bar.

He told the meeting that the passage of time had meant that it would not be possible to obtain an allocation of steel in time for building operations to begin before September 1957. However by February 1956 he had revised his plans yet again and details of the steel required had been sent to the Cleveland Bridge & Engineering Company. A member of the Property & Works Sub-Committee, Mr W. W. Hill-Wood, undertook to help in obtaining steel. Peacock hoped that if the steel could be ordered immediately, it would be possible after all to start building operations in the autumn. He did, however, perhaps with a feeling of relief, point out that the steel would have to be ordered before any tenders could be accepted for the main contract. Thus the Club would be committed to a definite order, and it would not be possible to consider further amendments to the basic design.

In August 1956 Peacock reported that tenders from eight building contractors had been received. The lowest, from Kirk & Kirk Ltd, was for £110,886, excluding fees and seats. Peacock considered this to be reasonable in view of the increases in the costs of labour, steel and bar equipment, and the need for additional site works and drainage. He proposed that the work should be undertaken in two stages, but after what was described as long and careful discussion at the next meeting, it was recommended that the work should proceed under one contract throughout the 1957 cricket season in order that the stand could be completed as soon as possible and with some saving in cost. The architect gave an assurance that approximately 800 seats would be available throughout the season.

Although Peacock did not think that the employment of a clerk of works was essential, he did feel that it would be desirable for the Club's own Clerk of Works, Mr G. Valentine, to act in a supervisory capacity. The Sub-Committee accepted this, providing that these new duties did not interfere with his existing work. It was recommended that a bonus should be paid to him for this appointment.

The Sub-Committee felt that the proposed cost of tip-up seats – approximately £15,000 – was much too high, and asked Aird, the Secretary, to obtain estimates for the normal type of seats used at the ground, which a year earlier had been priced at only a little over £7,000. At the next meeting, at the end of October, Aird reported that Wrinch of Ipswich, who had already supplied a large quantity of the seats at Lord's, had constructed a special hardwood seat with galvanised steel supports for consideration. The cost would be no more than £5 per unit, each of which would

accommodate four people, as compared to £10 per seat allowed for in the contract, thus saving nearly £4,000.

It was decided to incorporate some twenty feet of the gardens of 8 and 12 Elm Tree Road into the ground (there being no number 10), and to rebuild the boundary wall at this point. The site works would also include a new road at the back of the stand and a new grass mound to replace the one the stand would cover.

Kirk & Kirk started promptly in September 1956. In October the work progressed satisfactorily, and Valentine was granted an interim bonus of £150, with the promise of a further £100 to be paid on completion. Shortly after, there was an engineering strike and delays at the Cleveland Bridge & Engineering Company. The steelwork, which should have been delivered in February, and erected before the start of the season, was delayed. It was not welded and in place until the middle of May 1957.

In April, at the request of the Treasurer, the Sub-Committee was brought up to date with the financial position. The original contract sum was £104,452, and the original overall estimate approved by the MCC Committee, £124,708. This had now risen to £127,823. At the same meeting the decision was taken, reluctantly, to fell the plane tree at the rear of the stand. This was a highly-regarded feature of this part of the ground, and the planning authority wanted to see it retained, but there was evidence that the site works had damaged its roots.

In June there was a further setback. Some of the prefabricated reinforced-concrete steps were found to be sub-standard, and the architect ordered the contractor to replace them all. By October the work was back on course, and it looked as though completion would be by the end of the year. Valentine was voted a further interim bonus of £150. The Sub-Committee approved, subject to some amendments, a sketch, drawn by Christopher Ironsides and

Top: The back of the Warner Stand seen from Carriage Mound.

Bottom: Sir Pelham Warner (right), invited by the Duke of Norfolk, President, to open the stand on 7 May 1958.

based on an early print in the ownership of the Club, which would form a mural in the Members' Bar.

The stand was finished in the spring of 1958. A steel mainframe had been used in preference to reinforced concrete, due to the difficulties of weathering and maintenance that the Club was encountering with the stands designed by Baker. The contractors had used an all-welded system with a minimum of bolted connections, and all steelwork was exposed for painting and stood proud of the surrounding brickwork, which was of eleven-inch, cavity-wall construction. The main cantilevers were fabricated in three sections, with site welds across the full width of the section in two places. The cantilever frames are stiffened laterally by tubular bracketing and portal framing in the two bays at each end of the stand.

The ground terracing is in situ concrete, and the upper terracing has steel plate risers bolted to the main frame, with precast concrete slabs and in situ topping. The roof is of aluminium decking on steel channel purlins, with two-layer felt finish and a layer of insulation boards topped with white spar chips. The engineers for the scheme were R. T. James & Partners.

The stand was built on four levels. In the basement there is a beer cellar, a wine store and a hoist. At ground level the terraces seat 1,354, and there is a bar and WCs. At the first upper level, which is really a mezzanine floor, is the members' bar, a store room and men's toilets. On the top level there is terracing to seat 1,481 on each side and in front of the Press box. This had accommodation for radio and television commentators, as well as for nearly 100 members of the Press.

On 6 June 1958 *The Builder* reported the official opening of the stand on 7 May by Sir Pelham Warner, after whom it had been named, and the Duke of Norfolk, President of MCC. *The Builder* described the structure as 'a handsome and new building which fits well into the existing scheme'.

In her book *Lord's 1946–70* Diana Rait Kerr reported:

> The bar/cafeteria on the first floor has fine picture windows . . . and the 'mod cons' are a great improvement. It was only the other day that I learned from an old friend that in the 'conveniences' to which gentlemen may retire, the usual fittings are each furnished with a window through which the cricket may be watched. 'How old Plum would have loved this,' said my friend to his neighbour. 'I bet the old boy thought of it himself,' was the reply. Whoever the planning genius may have been, I need hardly add that he did not extend this particular piece of planning to the nose-powdering accommodation provided for ladies, which is sited discreetly at the rear so as to preclude any possibility of keeping in touch with the game.

The members of the fourth estate and the radio and television commentators, who had become attached to their rather primitive space at the top of the Pavilion, had mixed views about their accommodation. The sound-proofed and altogether better-appointed space in the new stand had the disadvantage of not affording a view from behind the bowler's arm. E. W. Swanton, writing in the *Daily Telegraph*, said:

> I was, it so happened, the last cricket writer ever to put pen to paper in the place where the game had been written about for half a century. For the new stand, which will be completed before next season, includes Press accommodation, built into the back of the upper storey. The appointments will be far superior, in keeping with modern requirements, although the angle will be less satisfactory. So passes the old box where the Pardons reigned supreme, where one remembers as a young man being appropriately awed by Charles Stewart Caine, where Neville Cardus was at first too shy to enter.

Now, half a century on, the commentators and the writers have moved again, to the Media Centre, at the opposite end of the ground and back in line with the wickets. The former Press box in the Warner Stand is empty and awaits the refurbishment of the stand to plans prepared by David Morley Architects.

13

The Houses – Opportunity Lost

1880–1990

The rectangle of land of which Lord's is part is enclosed by roads. Thomas Lord's original 1813 lease of about 8.25 acres was in the centre of the block, and once the Club had purchased the freehold in 1866, the Committee was far-sighted enough to realise that its goal should be to acquire the balance of the land within the rectangle. This was achieved, finally, in 1929. Sadly, the enormous benefit that this could have brought by enabling MCC to extend the ground was lost through lack of vision and short-term financial considerations in the years following the Second World War. But the history of the buildings at Lord's cannot be complete without reference to the acquisition and loss of the houses.

In 1869 MCC was able to buy a strip of land on its eastern side called Guy's Garden. In 1887 – the Club's centenary year – it bought the three-and-a-half acres of Henderson's Nursery from the Clergy Orphan Foundation for £18,500. Then in 1891 the Clergy Female Orphan School had been acquired from the Manchester & Sheffield Railway in exchange for the right to tunnel under the strip of land fronting Wellington Road. In 1880 MCC bought J. H. Dark's house in St John's Wood Road, and in 1894 the freeholds of 43 and 45 St John's Wood Road, just to the east of the tennis court. With these purchases the Club became the owner of all the island site except for the houses on the north and west sides of the ground.

From 1880 the Club pursued a policy of acquiring these dwellings, but at the outbreak of the Great War seven still did not belong to MCC, and five of those were in a single ownership. In 1921, 14 Elm Tree Road was bought, and in 1925, 8 Grove End Road. Meanwhile, in 1922, when the Grace Gates were being planned, Herbert Baker designed new luncheon rooms in the garden of 2 Grove End Road, and the house, which was in poor condition, was demolished. The Committee instructed 'that the ground where the old house formerly stood should be cleared, levelled, and left in that condition for the present'.

In 1928 the Club was presented with the opportunity of acquiring the freehold interest in the remaining houses, 10, 12, 14 and 16 Grove End Road and 6 Elm Tree Road. On 4 March 1929 a Special General Meeting was convened to ask members to ratify the conditional contract. The President, Brigadier General the Earl of Lucan, explained that this proposed purchase, in the sum of £66,500, would complete the Club's ownership of property abutting Lord's from the corner of St John's Wood Road to 22 Elm Tree Road, behind the eastern end of the Grand Stand. It would, he said, 'considerably enhance the value of the freehold already owned by the Club, and would free the Club from the risk of an adverse owner erecting flats . . . which would overlook and spoil the amenities of the ground.'

He warned members that 'it was difficult to say at present how the properties might be utilised to advantage other than as dwelling houses, from which only a comparatively small return would be received, although higher rentals should be obtained in

Right: A plan of Lord's Ground in 1856, corrected to 1868, shows the strip of land known as Guy's Nursery acquired in 1869. The adjoining two houses were bought in 1894, while Dark's house, in the south-western corner of the Ground, had been acquired in 1880. Before the turn of the century MCC had acquired 1 and 3 Grove End Road (later numbered 2 and 6), and four of the houses on the south side of Elm Tree Road.

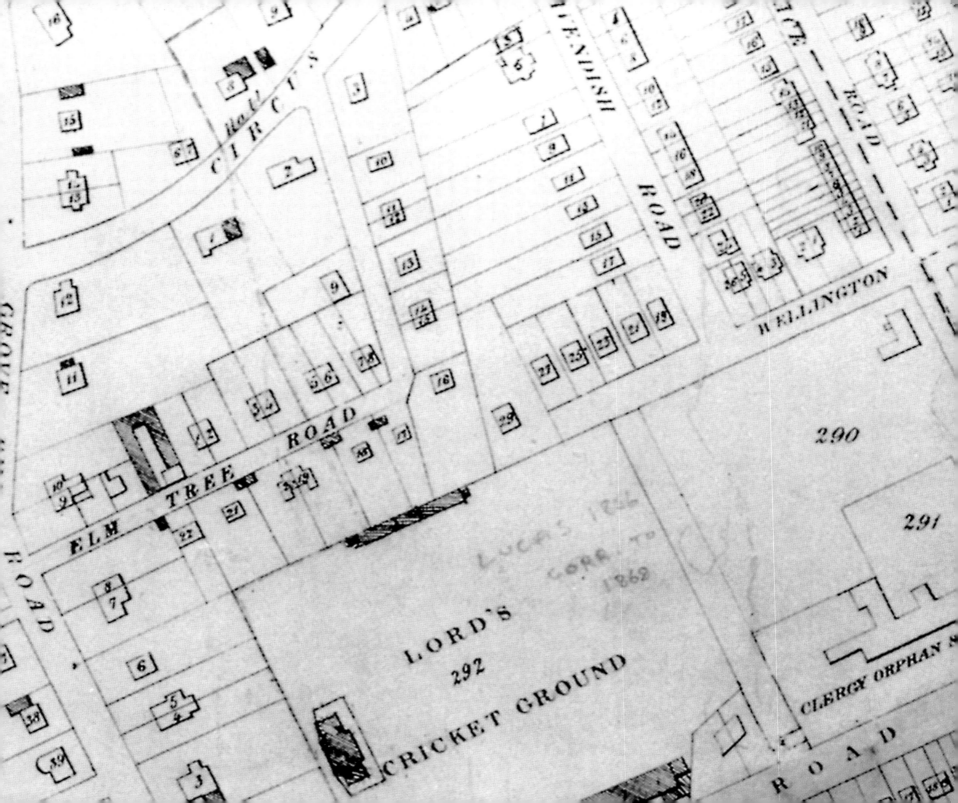

about three years' time when the leases of the present houses would expire.' It was, he said, 'impossible to foresee the growth of the Club, but it was quite certain that if the opportunity of purchasing the property now were lost, it would probably never occur again except at a considerably increased figure.' The members present agreed unanimously.

Thus the Secretary assumed responsibility for the management of an urban estate of fourteen houses, as well as of the Match and Practice Grounds and their buildings. The Committee received regular reports of new lettings, which were usually for seven years, and of the needs for repairs. In 1937, following the initiative of W. E. Ringland, the Club's agent, the Clerk of Works advised that 8 and 10 Grove End Road and 6, 8 and 12 Elm Tree Road should be rebuilt as soon as the leases came to an end. The Annual Report presented to members on 4 May 1938 warned that many of the Club's houses were old and that when some leases expired, rebuilding would be necessary. To finance this the Committee had set up a fund, transferring to it investments to the value of £25,000. (In 1950 that fund stood at £80,800.)

Mr Ringland thought the future of flats very doubtful, as they got out of date quickly, would be difficult to modernise, and the return on the capital would be inadequate. He felt that if the Club let the ground on building leases, it would ultimately lose the control which should be retained over the fringe properties against the possibility of the ground itself ever being developed, when exits to the boundary roads would become essential. He was strongly in favour of detached houses being built, to be let on repairing leases for periods of twenty-one years.

Late in 1938 Baker and Scott prepared a site plan for the layout of new houses on the land occupied by 6 to 14 inclusive Elm Tree

Road. This scheme was approved by the Committee and the LCC early in 1939. At much the same time the tenant of number 6 sought the Club's agreement to an early surrender of his lease. This was accepted, and Baker was asked to prepare detailed plans for a new house. The AGM in May 1939 was told that the rebuilding of the property, which was in a bad structural state, was about to be put in hand at a cost estimated at £5,500; but at the first meeting of the Emergency Committee on 11 September 1939 it was confirmed that the demolition and the plans to rebuild had been suspended.

In the air raids during the second half of 1940, the houses suffered considerably. 6 Grove End Road was virtually demolished, numbers 8 and 16 were rendered uninhabitable, and 4, 10, 12 and 14 were damaged. In December the Secretary's house, 22 Elm Tree Road, was slightly damaged. There was then a lull, until 6 Elm Tree Road was demolished by an incendiary bomb in March 1945, thus achieving what the Club had planned to do in 1939.

In January 1944 Baker was asked to revise the Clerk of Works' 1937 report on the houses. His findings in Grove End Road were:

2:     House demolished 1923: site covered with air raid shelters.

4:     Unoccupied: at least fifty per cent requires rebuilding.

6:     Demolished by enemy action: site partly occupied by a water tank.

8 & 10: A pair of semi-detached houses beyond repair.

12:    Vacant and needing considerable expenditure to make habitable.

14:    Occupied and not inspected.

16:    Badly damaged by a fire bomb in 1940, since when deterioration has occurred.

Right: The Ground in 1929, showing 18 and 14 Elm Tree Road, bought in 1910 and 1920 respectively. 4 and 8 Grove End Road were bought in 1912 and 1925. In 1929, 10, 12, 14 and 16 were bought, together with 6 Elm Tree Road.

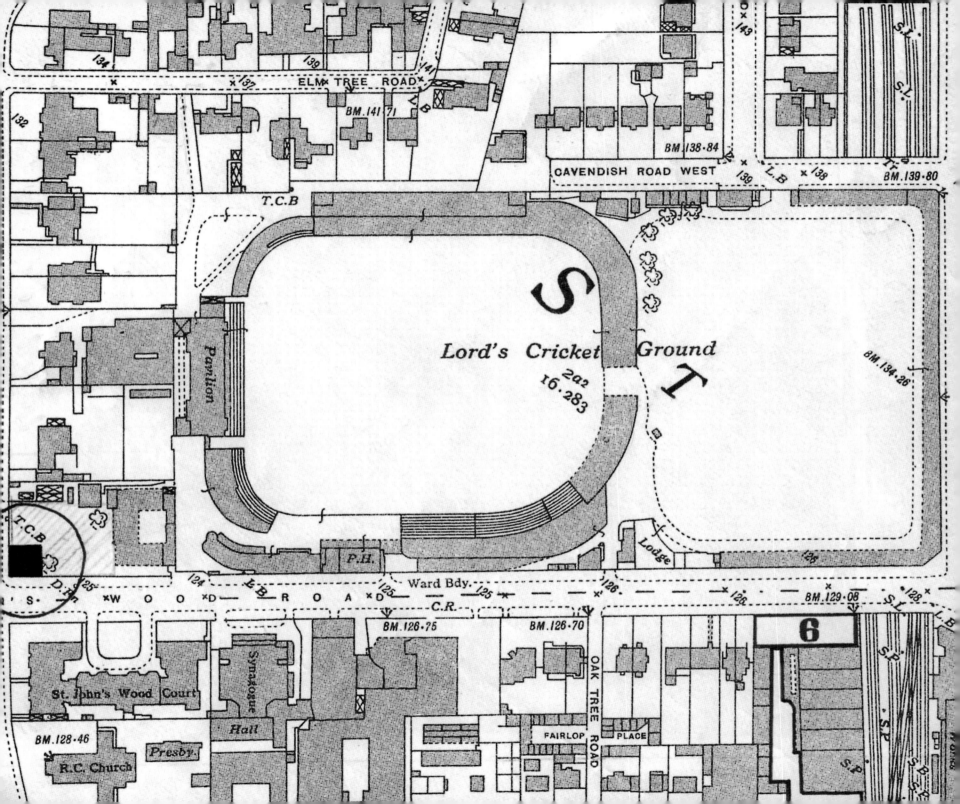

In March 1944 the General Purposes Sub-Committee agreed to recommend that Baker and Scott should prepare a rough plan for flats on the site of 4–10 Grove End Road, and that 12, 14 and 16 should be restored as houses. However, when Scott met committee members at the end of the month, the properties in Grove End and Elm Tree roads formed an important part of the discussion. The large house at 12 Grove End Road needed major expenditure to make it habitable, and it was agreed that it should be demolished. As for number 16, on the corner of the two roads, Baker's survey had found that the building needed to be reconditioned and the interior rearranged. The general feeling of the Committee was that it would be difficult to find a tenant for such a large house at a satisfactory rent, and that it should be demolished, thus leaving the whole of the Grove End frontage from 2 to 16 available for flats.

Scott wanted to demolish the tennis courts as well and extend the Harris Lawn for the full length of the Pavilion. Colonel Rait Kerr said that he agreed with the idea, but thought that the Committee would not endorse it as the tennis court was regarded as 'something of an ancient monument on the ground'.

Baker and Scott responded by preparing an ambitious scheme, which Scott later revised in April 1950, for the whole of the Grove End Road frontage. Their plans showed, on the corner of Grove End Road and St John's Wood Road, four shops with three flats above, with twenty flats on the rest of the site of number 2, together with the site of 4. In place of numbers 6 and 8 they designed an indoor cricket school with twelve flats over, and a small office block. There were to be twenty-five more flats on the site of numbers 10–16. The linked blocks were designed with a ground floor and five upper floors, and underground parking for sixty cars. The flats had red-brick, load-bearing walls under tiled roofs in the style typical of Lutyens' and Baker's domestic architecture of the 1930s. Although conditional permission for this scheme was received from the local panning authority, the plans were never implemented, perhaps because of the size and cost of the project.

In May 1951, when the LCC asked the Club to sell it 10–16 Grove End Road for building a primary school, MCC replied that the land was required for 'improvement of club amenities and future development proposals' and was not, therefore, for sale. In the same year the County of London Redevelopment Plan zoned the ground as a sports stadium, and the two lengths of frontage land as residential. The Club lodged an objection, stating that alternative proposals would be submitted as and when required.

Also in 1951, 6 Elm Tree Road, destroyed by enemy action, was rebuilt as a residence for an Assistant Secretary. In April 1952, six years after it had first been decided to demolish 16 Grove End Road, part of which was a dangerous structure, the decision was implemented. A licence was obtained to build a house for the newly-appointed second Assistant Secretary, S. C. Griffith, and an estimate was obtained from Dove Brothers Ltd in the sum of £5,833. The property is now called 4 Elm Tree Road.

The next month, the impending retirement of the Secretary, Colonel Rait Kerr, raised questions about the future of number 22, which was in a poor structural state. The house had started life as a small urban cottage and had been extended in every direction with large rooms, resulting in an inconvenient layout. The Secretary's successor, Ronald Aird, indicated that he wanted to stay in the next-door house, number 20, built for him to a design by Baker in 1939. After some delay in finding a tenant, number 22 was let. The Club eventually demolished the building in 1966, and three houses designed by the Louis de Soissons partnership were built on the site. They were sold on long leases, and two have been enfranchised so far.

The question of redevelopment in Grove End Road came finally to a head at a long joint meeting of the Property & Works and Town Planning Sub-Committees on 22 July 1953, with the decision to ask Louis de Soissons whether he would be prepared to accept instructions from the Club. By March 1954, when the joint meeting was reconvened, the tenant of number 10 had vacated the premises. It was decided that as the property was in a very poor state of repair, and could not be made habitable at a reasonable cost, the house should be demolished and the site included in the redevelopment scheme. Its neighbour, number 8, had been vacated and demolished in 1952 and was being used temporarily as a members' car park.

Members of the two sub-committees discussed with Mr Gorringe and D. M. Hodges of Louis de Soissons what form the redevelopment should take. It was considered as a general principle that houses should be built, rather than flats, but that it might be necessary to include a small block of flats on the corner site on the junction of Grove End Road and St John's Wood Road, to increase the density of development, so as to win planning approval. It was further decided that the site of 6 Grove End Road, which was shallow because of the presence of the tennis and racquets courts, should be retained for club purposes. It became, and has remained, a car park.

In considering the financial position, various alternatives were debated. If the houses were sold on sixty-year leases, the cost of development, less the premiums obtainable, was estimated at £24,000. But it was considered that twenty-one-year leases would be less vulnerable to future legislation. Although it would result in an estimated deficit of £36,000, it was the method recommended.

At the next joint meeting, in July 1954, two alternative schemes for the redevelopment of the land were submitted by Hodges. After some deliberation it was decided to proceed with the building of seven houses on the sites of part of 4, of 8, 10, and 12, and what remained of 16. Gorringe had suggested that the houses should be of two floors, about 2,200 square feet in floor area, with five bedrooms and two reception rooms. They should have garages, central heating and two bathrooms.

By the time of the next meeting in November 1954, Hodges had received planning permission, and by the following June tenders were in from six building contractors. Robert Hart & Co. had submitted the lowest at £64,812. The architect identified where some economies could be made and reduced the total cost of the scheme to about £60,000. On this basis he received authority to proceed, with a contractual completion date of 3 October 1956. The designs followed Gorringe's specification, and the houses were built in brick with roofs of interlocking tiles.

Later in the year, when the arrangements for marketing the dwellings were discussed, it was decided that members of MCC should be given the first option and that a notice to that effect should go out with Rover Ticket application forms to all members on 1 January 1956. It was agreed that each house should be let on a twenty-one-year, full-repairing lease at a rental of £250 per annum, and that a premium of £6,000 should be asked.

In spite of the contractor's assurances, building fell steadily behind schedule. In October the Sub-Committee recommended, for reasons not recorded, that each house should be sold on a sixty-year lease with premiums in the bracket £11,000 - £13,000. John D. Wood & Co. were appointed as MCC's agents, and they agreed to accept half-scale commission on any sale to a member of the Club.

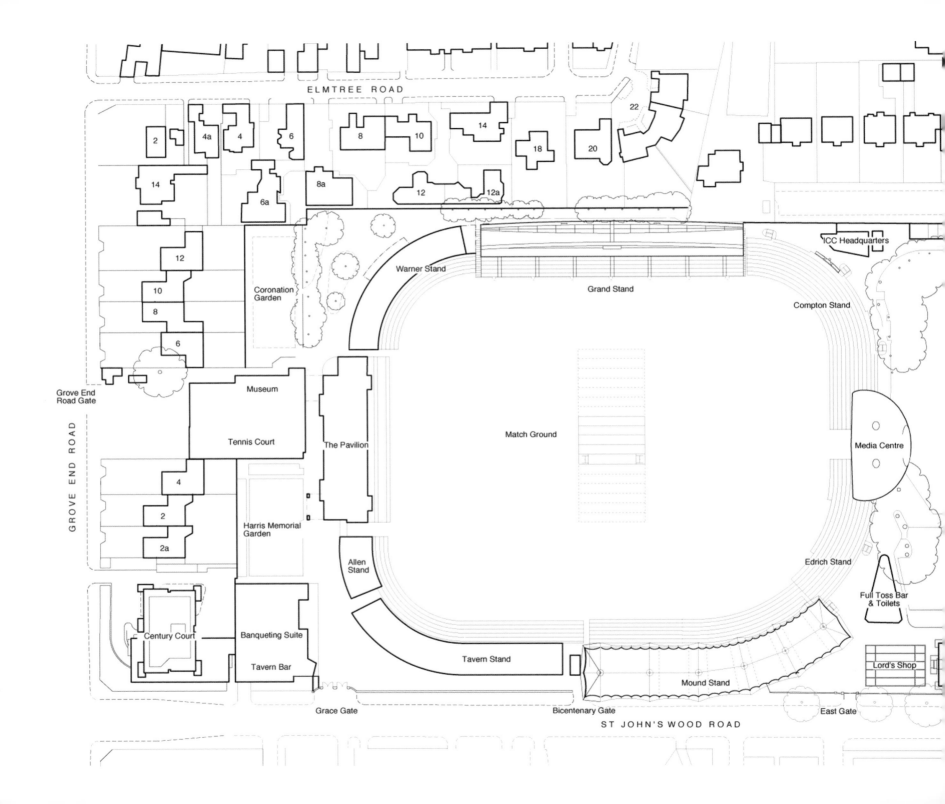

ELMTREE ROAD

2 4a 4 6 8 10 14

18 20 22

14

6a 8a 12 12a

12

Coronation Garden

Warner Stand

Grand Stand

Compton Stand

ICC Headquarters

10

8

6

Grove End Road Gate

GROVE END ROAD

Museum

Tennis Court

The Pavilion

Match Ground

Media Centre

4

2

2a

Harris Memorial Garden

Allen Stand

Edrich Stand

Full Toss Bar & Toilets

Century Court

Banqueting Suite

Tavern Bar

Tavern Stand

Mound Stand

Lord's Shop

Grace Gate

Bicentenary Gate

East Gate

ST JOHN'S WOOD ROAD

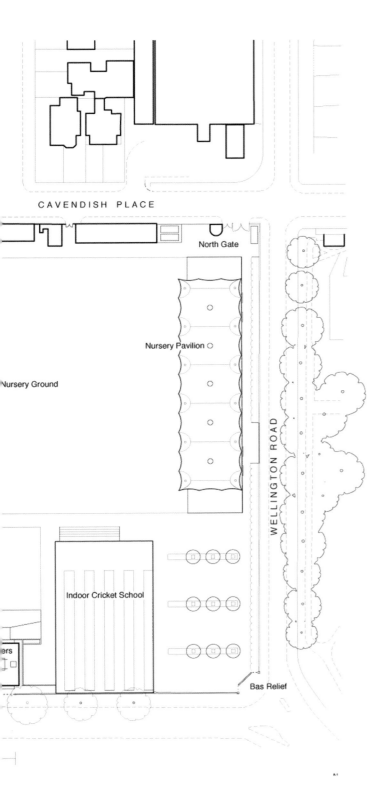

CAVENDISH PLACE

North Gate

Nursery Pavilion ○

Nursery Ground

WELLINGTON ROAD

Indoor Cricket School

ers

Bas Relief

In the end, the architect did not take over the new houses on behalf of the Club until 17 May 1957. Some members of the Sub-Committee inspected the properties and expressed themselves unhappy about the standard of finish. Hodges assured them that any defects would be put right, and by October 1957 all seven of the dwellings had been sold to members of the Club. The leases contained a covenant laying down that if the lessee should wish to sell his interest, it was to be offered to the Club in the first instance.

There remained a narrow plot at the southern end of Grove End Road, adjacent to the corner site which had been retained for flats. It was decided not to incorporate this land into the corner site, but to seek approval to build an eighth house. Hodges was asked to approach the planning authority, and by August 1958 he had received the necessary permission, together with an estimate for the cost of construction of £12,000. By the end of the following year the building had been completed, and a sixty-year lease at a ground rent of £100 per annum was sold for £14,500.

The reason for the change in the recommendation of the Property & Works Sub-Committee between February and October 1956, to sell the houses on the basis of sixty-year rather than twenty-one-year leases, is not spelled out in the Club minutes. It was presumably driven by advice that the premium obtainable for the longer lease was approximately twice what could have been obtained for the shorter one.

It was, and is, a tragedy for the Club that no one recalled the wise advice of Mr Ringland, MCC's estate agent, who in 1937 had warned that to sell long leases would lead to the Club losing control over fringe property, and deny it the ability to use the land for its own purposes. This had been reinforced by Munro Runtz, who advised that any new houses on the perimeter land should be

Left: A plan of the Ground in 2004.

let on twenty-one year leases, but in the end all this seems to have been forgotten.

In due course, under the provisions of the Leasehold Reform Act 1967, as amended, the owners of leases granted for terms in excess of twenty-one years became able, subject to certain conditions, to purchase the freehold interest in their properties. The owners of 2A, 2, 6, 8, 10 and 14 Grove End Road all took advantage of this. In 1990 number 4, the former home of 'Gubby' Allen, was bought by the Club from his estate for £450,000, and now is used as the residence of the Secretary. Number 12 is owned by the Cuban Government and is thus outside the provisions of the Act. Of course the Club has received capital payments on enfranchisement, but the opportunity to extend the ground has gone. It might have been otherwise.

14

The South-West Corner

1965–66

In the close season of 1965–66 the Secretary of MCC was in Australia, managing the touring team as it renewed its challenge for the Ashes. During his absence, the Committee at home was confronted with the biggest challenge the Club had ever faced.

The issue which, for the first time on record, threw into serious doubt the members' confidence in their Committee was the vast scheme for redeveloping the south-western corner of the ground, from Grove End Road to the Mound Stand. Few members, probably, had the sense of history to review the economic growth in the hundred years since Mr R. A. FitzGerald became Secretary (Honorary) of a comparatively modest club with no more than a few hundred members. To him, the capital reserves of more than £300,000 at the Committee's disposal in 1965 would have appeared inconceivable. Now the Committee was proposing to expend a sum equivalent to the whole of these reserves, achieved by years of good husbandry and shrewd investment, on massive plans to sweep away existing buildings, including the cherished Tavern and Clock Tower, and to transform this side of the ground by erecting a towering stand. In the light of declining attendances, a significant body of members regarded as an act of lunacy such prodigal expenditure on what might prove to be a white elephant.

Top: Demolition of Lord's Hotel in 1967 to make way for the Tavern Stand.

Bottom: The steel frame of the Tavern Stand rises from the ashes of Lord's Hotel.

A committee of finance and property experts had spent three years considering the development. The paramount necessity which activated and accelerated all other considerations was the obsolescence of the Tavern and its ancillary buildings as an effective control-centre for the Lord's catering. Since Mr Portman's day successive caterers had incurred annual losses amounting to five-figure sums, and now an experienced firm with all the resources of a large business was hardly more successful. It was clear that, under present conditions, Ring & Brymer would not renew their contract when it expired in 1967, and it was unlikely that any other professional caterer would be persuaded to take their place.

By the autumn of 1965 the Committee had approved well-integrated designs by David Hodges and Kenneth Peacock for the erection of flats, a new Tavern, and a stand which would engulf part of the old Q enclosure and continue around the perimeter of the ground as far as the Main Gate. The broad outline of these plans had appeared in the 1964 Annual Report, and members had been given fuller details in 1965. There was a warning of heavy capital expenditure and the likelihood of a rise in subscriptions. However, no estimates were given, and many members failed to appreciate fully the scope of the financial implications.

To forestall the probability of compulsory purchase, the first area to be considered had been the derelict Grove End Road corner site recently derequisitioned by the Water Board. Tenders were sought from contractor-developers to build a multi-storey block of flats, and early in 1965 it was agreed to accept W. T. Chown's offer of £150,000 for a ninety-nine-year lease for the right to erect a twelve-storey block of fifty-five flats and a penthouse, to plans approved by the Committee.

Left: The Upper Terrace taking shape.

Right: The New Tavern opened on 13 June 1967.

Faced with the imminent collapse of the catering, the Committee next accepted the necessity for building a new Tavern, and they bowed to the united advice of architects and catering experts that, as the old Tavern site afforded too little space for an effective catering unit, the new Tavern should be built immediately to the west of the Grace Gates and adjoining the new flats. In such a restricted space it was obvious that much time and money could be saved by having one contract for the flats and the Tavern. Chown's contract was therefore extended to include the construction of the Tavern with its 300-seater restaurant and large reception-room/cafeteria, at a cost to MCC estimated at £140,000. In round terms, therefore, the flats were to pay for the Tavern. Hodges was the architect for both.

A decision had now to be made about the fate of the old Tavern, with the adjoining Members' Dining-room and the Clock Tower, whose boxes, behind their charming wrought-iron balustrades, had been honoured by the presence of kings and queens, prime ministers, and the most illustrious figures in the British Commonwealth. Sentiment and affection were overwhelmingly on the side of conservation, for to pull them down was to drop the curtain for ever on romantic rendezvous under the Clock, to silence the bucolic 'Old Met' humorists on the Tavern promenade, and to deprive loyal Taverners of their home.

Economy as well as sentiment seemed to argue for their preservation, adapted as far as practicable for bars and cafeteria. But practicality was the key to the argument for demolition. Preserving the shells of these buildings would have involved heavy outlay on conversion and repairs to crumbling fabric, for an end-product of limited functional value. As for the Clock Tower, it was doomed already by the plans for the new Tavern, which involved side-stepping the Grace Gates thirteen feet to the east, thus making the Tower an obstacle in the way of a dignified driveway up to the Pavilion.

The Committee concluded, not without heart-searching, that it would be false economy to pour money into the sieve represented by obsolete buildings, and thereby abandon an opportunity of completing the modernization of the ground, which might be lost for ever. So it now approved, as the third stage, Peacock's four-decker stand, in which the needs of Taverners would be met by a fine concourse and bar. The remainder of the ground-level terrace and the top tier was designed for members and their friends (to support a larger membership), and the two middle tiers provided twenty large twenty-four-seater boxes with moveable partitions to convert each to two smaller units if desired.

By the members' assent at successive annual meetings, the Committee had a mandate to go ahead with the plans and to enter contractually into an agreement, but the members' approval at a special general meeting was needed to secure the 'ways and means'. This meeting was held at Lord's on 20 October 1965 with a threefold agenda: to ratify the sale of the tender of the building-lease of ninety-nine years to Chown; to authorise the Trustees to sell investments and exercise their powers of borrowing to the extent necessary to implement the proposals; and to increase the number of full members and raise the annual subscription rates by fifty per cent, from £6 to £9 for full members and from £4 to £6 for Associate members.

As was customary, the meeting was summoned by notices in *The Times* and the *Daily Telegraph*, but a body of members complained that there had been insufficient notice and that, on such complicated issues, a full written explanation should have been given. A notice inserted by a member in the personal column of *The Times*, urging members to attend, 'to oppose the proposals to provide funds for [this] grandiose building programme', foretold that this meeting would be no formal rubber-stamping of the Committee's proposals.

Those who attended heard a lucid explanation of the plans from the President, Sir Oliver Leese, supported by the Treasurer and G. C. Newman and M. J. C. Allom, Chairmen respectively of the sub-committees responsible for redevelopment and catering. The first resolution, ratifying the sale of the building lease for the flats, was passed by a substantial majority, but on the other two an amendment was carried demanding that a second special general meeting be convened in writing, giving twenty-one days' notice, accompanied by an explanation of the Committee's proposals. The feeling of the meeting was that, regardless of the merits of these two resolutions, they should be referred back on the grounds that members had received insufficient information and that the announcement of the meeting had not been seen by enough members to secure a representative attendance.

Such a barrage of criticism aimed at an establishment hitherto unchallenged did not pass unnoticed by the Press. In the *Daily Mail* Alex Bannister drew a word-picture of the President, General Leese, and his staff with their backs to the Long Room wall. It is fair to say that the Committee was considerably shaken by the strength of the opposition, and meticulous preparations were made for the second meeting, convened for 1 January 1966. A booklet explained every aspect of the scheme, with descriptions, plans and drawings of the new buildings and estimates of cost. The required capital, £305,000, could have been met from the resources of the MCC Trust Fund but, rather than absorb all of the Club's readily-realisable assets, the Committee proposed to raise a third from the sale of investments and to borrow the balance on a bank loan repayable over thirty years.

Finally, there was an explanation of the proposed new structure for subscriptions and membership, which was designed to provide substantial additional income to cover the loss of revenue from investments and the cost of servicing the loan, and leave a balance to meet rising costs. The standard subscriptions were raised by fifty per cent, but a concessionary rate was introduced for 'country' members living outside a radius of a hundred miles from Hyde Park Corner and for members under twenty-five or over sixty-five years old, whose subscriptions remained at the old rate. The addition of 1,000 Associate members and the election of full members up to the permitted maximum of 10,000 by January 1967 promised a new total of 14,000.

Some 750 members had notified their intention to attend (though no more than 550 turned up). Such a throng exceeded the capacity of the Long Room, and the venue was transferred to the more commodious Seymour Hall, where formality was added to the occasion by the elevation of the Committee and its advisers to a platform raised well above the floor of the hall. News had just been received of England's victory in the third Test, and in his opening speech the President referred to it, saying:

> The reputation and standing of Lord's is second to none in cricketing circles in the world. It is the Mecca of cricketers of all nations and the headquarters of cricket from which come forth the Laws of Cricket, the spirit in which it should be played, and the encouragement to men of all ages and all nations to play what we believe to be the finest game of all. And what better example than the manner in which our team have gone about their tour from the moment they set foot in Australia, bringing them this brilliant victory today? Would you like me to send a telegram of congratulations from this meeting to the team?

The back of the Tavern Stand seen from the Grace Gates.

The completed Tavern Stand.

Needless to say, whatever disagreements there may have been about the formal resolutions on the agenda, this impromptu resolution was passed with acclamation. The President went on to plead that, if MCC were to maintain its prestige, it must move with the times and provide accommodation, buildings, catering facilities, and Match and Practice Grounds second to none. This was a wonderful opportunity for MCC to show that it had faith in the game of cricket and in the future of Lord's.

Again there were three resolutions. The first concerned the Trustees' powers of borrowing and charging the property and assets of the Club to the extent necessary to implement the redevelopment. The other two resolutions sought approval for the new subscription and membership structure. The main debate focused on Resolution One. The plans for the flats and the Tavern were accepted almost without demur, but there was lively criticism of the proposed outlay on the stand. The President and the Chairman of the Redevelopment Sub-committee explained the reasons why the Committee had hastened to sign an agreement in April, foreseeing accurately new legislation which would otherwise have necessitated building licences. The nature of the scheme, with every part of the operation dovetailing into another, was so highly integrated that it had been essential to have a single contract for the whole.

The most extreme opposition came from a group of members whose amendment excluded altogether the rebuilding and modernization of the Clock Tower and Tavern, specifically limiting the Trustees' powers to raising money for the new Tavern.

The completed Tavern Stand filled with members and their friends in 1968.

However, this amendment was heavily defeated. It was pointed out that failure to build the stand now would attract a claim for breach of contract of not less than £20,000, to which must be added £7,750 for fees. The demolition of the Clock Tower, with the consequent loss of its boxes and 500 seats above, could not be avoided if the Tavern project was accepted, so only the old Tavern and Members' Dining Room would remain. The transformation of these buildings into a viable proposition by extensive repairs, new drainage, and conversion would bring the total cost of retaining them to well over £50,000, without taking account of the loss of income from the Clock Tower and a sizeable reduction in the new catering contract offered by Watney, Mann.

The subsequent debate, well argued on both sides, devolved upon the enormous cost of the stand, which its critics said was out of all proportion to the Club's requirements. The day was won by Sir Bernard Waley-Cohen, whose well-reasoned amendment asked that consideration be given to a modified new stand, costing less than the £280,000 at present envisaged.

In order to adhere to the building programme the Committee now had to act fast to consider possible modifications. On the very day after the meeting it considered whether to omit the top terrace, thus saving £20,000 at the expense of 1,500 seats, or whether to limit the boxes to one tier, saving £33,600 and losing twenty boxes and their revenue. It chose the latter, and aesthetically this improved the stand whose additional height would otherwise have dwarfed all other buildings on the ground.

Left: The Members' Bar with views over the ground.

Right: The back of the bar showing the mural by Christopher Ironsides.

Work on the flats began without making any profound impact on Lord's. Now, in the spring, the first visible sign that the main development was about to start was the re-siting of the Grace Gates. Work on the Tavern block, scheduled for completion in 1967, was screened behind a lofty barrier. The destruction of the old Tavern and Clock Tower began only after Lord's had closed its gates to the last spectator in the autumn, and there were few to witness the sorry devastation and feel the sharp nostalgic pang as these well-loved buildings crumbled before the might of bulldozers.

The day fixed for the formal opening of the new Tavern was 13 June 1967, a week before the Test match against India. Mr Griffith drew the first pint, as he had drawn the last in the old Tavern the previous autumn.

Once the demolition squads had done their worst, some semblance of order emerged above the barricades which hid the new stand. From time to time huge pre-cast units rose up into the sky, hovered, and then settled as the phoenix arose from the ashes. The stand was ready on schedule for the second Australian Test in 1968, and there were moments before the notorious hailstorm blanched the ground, concentrating its carpet in front of the stand, when its occupants basked in glorious sun. As a viewpoint for watching the cricket, the boxes are a vast improvement on their predecessors, for they are less remote than the Clock Tower and, whether you are an avid watcher or prefer to engage in social chatter, they are a great deal more comfortable. But such a fine structure is far too little used.

15

The Mound Stand

1984–87

Pictures of the ground from the late nineteenth century show the Pavilion dominating the scene: it appears massive and solid, with its shaded verandas floating airily over the heavy base. The subsequent perimeter development, which changed Lord's from a village ground into a cricket arena, was haphazard.

The first of the raked enclosures was the original Mound Stand, designed by Frank Verity in 1898 and built at the south-eastern corner of the ground, on the site of the first Tennis Court. To begin with, it was conceived in a majestic and stylish form. Verity wanted to support the terraces on a colonnade of brick arches, and intended that his scheme should provide an elegant model for enclosing the entire ground. Sadly, funds were not forthcoming, and only seven of the proposed arches were completed. The rest of the terrace was supported on a basic, inelegant steel structure. Nevertheless, for the next seventy years the Mound became an integral feature of the Lord's scene and, despite its appearance, was a popular place from which to watch the cricket, particularly in the late afternoon, when spectators were bathed in evening sunshine.

The completion of the Tavern Stand in 1968 left the Club in a tight financial situation, because costs had been higher than

The original seven arches of the Mound Stand, designed by Frank Verity in 1898, but seen here in about 1965.

expected, and for the next decade attitudes to expenditure could best be described as cheese-paring. The result was a patch-and-mend policy, and the whole estate fell into disrepair. Lord's, in fact, deteriorated into a shameful condition. The only repairs authorised were carried out by the Works Department under the supervision of the Clerk of Works, Mr Ted Collins, who did a good job within the confines of the limited funds made available.

Then in 1979 Colin Stansfield-Smith (the County Architect for Hampshire) was appointed Chairman of the Property & Works Sub-Committee. He and his colleagues managed, by persistent and well-argued recommendations, to persuade the main Committee that their stingy policy was having a disastrous effect on the fabric of the estate.

After a major change in attitude, the first signs of recovery began to appear on the Pavilion. Many of the ugly excrescences were removed, and several rooms which had been taken over as offices were returned to members' use. Although it took some

time for the benefits of the new policy to become apparent, it is reasonable to say that the transformation of Lord's into an architectural showpiece began from this time.

It was with this background that, in August 1984, David Male took over the reins as Chairman of the newly-named Estates Sub-Committee and assumed responsibility for the construction of a new stand, to be ready for the Club's bicentenary celebrations in 1987. Male quickly assembled a Working Party to oversee the project. Apart from himself as Chairman, this consisted of Peter Bell, John Gasson, Brian Thornton and Paul Wates, with Lieutenant Colonel Leslie James as Secretary.

The Working Party decided to invite five practices to compete for the appointment of architect, and the challenge was thrown down in February 1985, when five firms were asked to submit designs for a new building to replace the old Verity stand, an honorarium of £1,000 being paid to each.

Colin Stansfield-Smith, who had been co-opted to assist the Working Party, was most persuasive in his support for the scheme put up by Michael Hopkins & Partners. Peter Bell, himself an architect, made an impassioned plea and demonstrated why Hopkins's solution was so outstandingly the best. He showed that it was the only design which proposed to retain the existing terrace – a solution that made particular sense, given the tight schedule, if the stand was to be ready for the 1987 season. He explained that it was the only design that incorporated a fabric roof, with its symbolism of festival cricket in England.

The sketches that Hopkins produced with his submission also revealed a profound understanding of Lord's, and of the importance of building on its traditions. He emphasised the value, as he saw it, of not turning the arena into yet another stadium. His concept was that Lord's should remain essentially a cricket

Concept drawing illustrating the arcade
beneath the refurbished terrace.

ground, with separate pavilions surrounding it and views into the playing area between each building. The Working Party was convinced, and Hopkins was appointed in March 1985.

In September that year the budget for the overall cost was set at £3 million, but the Finance Committee was most concerned that the Club could not possibly commit itself to such expenditure – and it was at this point that John Paul Getty II came to the rescue. The philanthropist's interest in cricket had been sparked off by his friendship with Mick Jagger, and fostered by an introduction to Colin Cowdrey, the Kent and England captain. Through his adviser, the art dealer Christopher Gibbs, Getty made it known that he would like to do something for Lord's – and so it was that he met Christopher's brother Roger, who was on the MCC Committee and Chairman of the City institution Gerrard & National. When shown the design for the Mound Stand, Getty admired it and said he would like to help.

'Go and see my accountant at Deloitte's,' he instructed.

Together, Sir Anthony Tuke, MCC Treasurer, and Gibbs told the accountant what the cost of the Mound Stand was forecast to be. Sir Anthony said he felt it was appropriate for the MCC members to find half this sum, but they were looking for the balance of £1.5 million. The immediate response was: 'I know Mr Getty would like to provide the other half. Would it be possible to pay £1 million at the end of the month, and the other £500,000 in six months' time?'

'It certainly would!' Sir Anthony replied. The project was on.

When tenders were sought, Higgs and Hill proved the most competitive firm, and were appointed management contractors. The retention of the existing terrace allowed construction work to be split into two winter phases. The first phase began in September 1985, with the removal of the outbuildings and the old

Seen from St John's Wood Road, the arches marching along the back of the stand replicate the scheme envisaged by Frank Verity in 1898. They also present a much more interesting façade to the street than the stand's predecessor.

Bottom left: The Bicentenary Gates behind the Mound Stand, given by the Duke of Westminster in memory of his uncle, the Viscount Cobham.

Bottom right: The arcade beneath the stand, where spectators visit the bars and enjoy the protection of the stand above while meeting friends.

steel and corrugated-iron roof, which was soon achieved. The foundations for the superstructure were installed, and the Verity arcade was extended down the St John's Wood side of the refurbished terrace. Through the colonnade's development, St John's Wood Road regained some of the varied character it had before the Lord's Tavern was demolished. The views through the brick arches and their elegant new railings also now satisfy the curiosity of passers-by, who, for many years, had been unable to see what happened behind the forbidding perimeter wall.

Great care was taken to maintain the integrity of Verity's brickwork design, and load-bearing brickwork was used for the new extension of the rudimentary colonnade. The bricks were London Stocks, recovered from an old tent manufacturer's factory in Camberwell, which dated from 1857 and had been

demolished. The decaying steel columns of the old stand were incorporated within new brick arches and left to rot away safely. The best bricks were used on the exterior of the arches, with common flettons being used on the inside.

Throughout the 1986 season the stand was used in its topless form. Because of the phased nature of the construction, it was inevitable that the first completed parts of the building would be subject to critical scrutiny, while the remaining part was still on the drawing board.

In the spring of 1986, as the newly-extended brick colonnade emerged from beneath the scaffolding, Hopkins, who had hitherto been neatly pigeon-holed as a high-tech architect, was accused by critics of having 'turned the clock back a century'. This accusation assumed greater irony in view of the praise received by

the MCC for having backed such a 'daring' design. However, once the superstructure was completed, it became clear that Hopkins had achieved a remarkable marriage of two technologies.

The construction of the first phase had caused the Working Party considerable anxiety, for progress was much slower than planned. It was touch and go whether the terrace would be ready for use for the first major match of the 1986 season. Consequently the Working Party decided that the contractor should appoint a new senior manager to oversee the much more complex works in the second phase. Higgs & Hill appointed Bob Oliver to undertake this difficult task.

It was during the winter of 1985 that Hopkins developed the design of the superstructure in collaboration with the structural engineers, Ove Arup . The prefabrication of the steelwork and the

fabric roof progressed throughout the summer of that year, but the specification of the actual material to be employed for the membrane of the roof had caused a particular problem.

Hopkins had originally recommended a Teflon (PTFE)-coated, woven glass-fibre fabric – a material which has a comparatively long life and is also self-cleaning. Unfortunately, at the time, the Department of the Environment placed a hold on its use for such a large project, until the fire risk and its potential toxicity in a fire had been further researched. (This was despite the fact that Teflon had been used on many buildings of this size throughout the world.) Eventually it was decided to use a polyester fabric coated in PVC with a fluoropolymer topcoat – a material with a life expectancy of fifteen years. When it is replaced, the Estates Committee will be able to give further consideration to the use of the materials that have been developed in the meantime.

The new Mound Stand was one of the first major stands to be commissioned after the Bradford fire disaster in 1985. In July 1985 and January 1986, Sir Oliver Popplewell produced post-Bradford reports, the recommendations of which had to be incorporated into the design. These involved the introduction of fire-alarms, smoke-detectors, emergency lighting and new railings at a late stage in the design process.

The prefabricated steel frame was erected in the second phase, and the superstructure was complete in time for the 1987 bicentenary season, but the fitting-out lagged behind, and unfortunately some parts of the building were not ready for occupation when the Duke of Edinburgh came to open the stand and attend the first day of the Bicentenary Test match on 6 May.

The opening ceremony took place just inside the new Bicentenary Gates located in the boundary wall behind the stand.

Left: The upper promenade, where debenture holders enjoy the light, festive atmosphere under the tented roof.

These new gates had been given to the Club by the Duke of Westminster in memory of his uncle, the Viscount Cobham, a past Treasurer and President of MCC. For many years there had been a sliding wooden gate at that point in the wall which, rather incongruously, had been known as the Main Gate. The new gates were much grander and more in keeping with the adjacent arches that now formed the boundary wall at the back of the new stand.

At the 1987 AGM, held on the same day, David Male came in for some criticism from members because costs had exceeded budget by nearly £1.3 million, but he was able to point out the considerable enlargement of the building that had been sanctioned during the design stage in order to provide the additional accommodation at the mezzanine level.

Meanwhile, Roger Gibbs had been given the somewhat tricky task of telling Paul Getty that the final cost had soared to £4.35 million. He said that MCC was not looking for anything further from their benefactor, but felt it only right that he should be put fully in the picture as to how the project had progressed and the cost had escalated.

Getty's immediate response was, 'I said I wanted to provide fifty per cent of the cost. You'll get a cheque for £650,000 next week.' Not only did he produce his half-share: he also took one of the new boxes in the stand, insisted on paying for it in full, and kept it on until his death in 2003.

The brilliant design of the completed building makes it appear that the superstructure floats airily above the old brickwork terrace with a grace that echoes Verity's Pavilion roof, but surpasses it in its scope and elegance. Despite the vast span of the structure, running across the entire terrace, just six steel columns support it, thus providing the 4,500 spectators seated below with unobstructed views and superb sightlines. The superstructure is based on a plate box-girder construction, tied down at eighteen-metre centres. Hanging from the girders are twenty-seven boxes, all with clear views of the playing area. They are set out, in a continuous row, on the same grid as the brick arches below.

Above the boxes the architect and engineer showed good spatial and structural ingenuity. Within the main box-girder framework, a mezzanine level was created, which was used to house lavatories, bar cellars and catering stores. Thus the walls of the lavatories are finished in painted steel, giving them a distinctly nautical atmosphere.

Rising above this, and under the tented membranes of the roof, is the upper promenade deck. Here is a space of quite outstanding quality. The light permeating the roof, and the breezes that flow across the area, engender the aura of a marquee beside the village green. There are bars and restaurants for the debenture holders, and the views from this level are superb, both of the pitch and of the surrounding cityscape. Up at this height, sixty feet above the ground, the building has a fair-weather character. The enclosure is not water-tight, and when it rains, drops tend to blow in; but if the weather turns really foul and rain stops play, spectators can remain dry by abandoning their exposed seats and seeking sanctuary in one of the stand's many bars.

The new Mound Stand has earned broad popular acclaim. The key to its success is that, by a skilful combination of architectural flair and engineering expertise, Hopkins united the usually-conflicting doctrines of conservation and modernism. This dramatic pavilion harks back to eighteenth-century cricket grounds, when there were marquees on the boundary to provide shelter for spectators and scorers. Hopkins has managed to bring off a remarkably clever sleight of hand by producing a modern building that reminds us of the past.

North elevation with the lift tower and clock visible above the old Mound Stand Scoreboard.

Since its completion it has become extraordinarily well-respected and liked, among not only architects and critics, but also the general public. It is one of the relatively few modern buildings to receive the approval of the Prince of Wales.

Left: The Mound Stand on completion in 1987, filled with spectators watching the Bicentenary Test match.

16

The Compton and Edrich Stands

1988–91

The acclaim which the new Mound Stand received marked a further turning-point in the attitude of the MCC Committee towards the upkeep and modernisation of Lord's. After some initial criticism, it soon became clear that the new stand was a resounding success both aesthetically and functionally. It also proved that good design paid handsomely, both in terms of the return on the investment and of the reputation of the Club. For example, the boxes and debenture seats were immediately in demand at the asking price; it would not be long before the cash borrowed to fund the building work was repaid.

With new-found confidence the Committee turned its attention to G and H Stands. Completed in 1924 to a design by Herbert Baker, these enclosed the ground at the Nursery End. The gap between them, which had been left open to allow maintenance machinery to be brought onto the pitch, had, for some unknown reason, been located off the centreline of the Pavilion. Known for many years as 'the Free Seats', the lower terraces provided some of the most dreadful conditions for watching cricket that could be found. The upper terrace had been designed with only 7 ft 6 ins of headroom

for the spectators below. Baker told the Committee that 'the back row would have a view of the game as far as the bottom of the Pavilion rails'; the fact that people would be unable to see any high balls did not seem to be a concern.

By 1987 it had become clear to J. J. Warr, the President, and the Committee that redevelopment could provide a significant increase in public seating and a great improvement in comfort and sight-lines. In 1988 the Estates Sub-Committee was asked to come forward with proposals. Little did anyone realise what a chapter of disasters would follow. No other redevelopment project at Lord's in recent years has given rise to such heartache.

In August 1988 an initial briefing was attended by Michael Hopkins (the appointed architect), Gubby Allen (a past-President of MCC) and David Male (Chairman of the Estates Sub-Committee). It was made clear to Hopkins that the view from the Pavilion of the trees behind the stands, and beyond in St John's Churchyard, was highly valued: he was left in no doubt that the Committee would not accept any design which compromised the prospect.

Soon after the meeting, Male reconstituted the Working Party that had been responsible for the Mound Stand redevelopment. Their brief to Hopkins was to maximise the number of seats within the existing footprint of G and H stands, and also within the height-restriction imposed by the main Committee. It was also suggested that the number of columns supporting the upper terraces should be minimised. Good sight-lines to the playing area and the comfort of spectators were to be high priority.

After Hopkins had prepared his first sketch designs, Clyde Malby, a partner in Davis, Belfield & Everest, who had acted as quantity surveyor for the Mound Stand project, advised MCC that it should budget for the cost of the two new stands at about £3.75

G and H stands showing the very low headroom between the upper and lower terraces. The gap between the stands was not on the centre line of the ground.

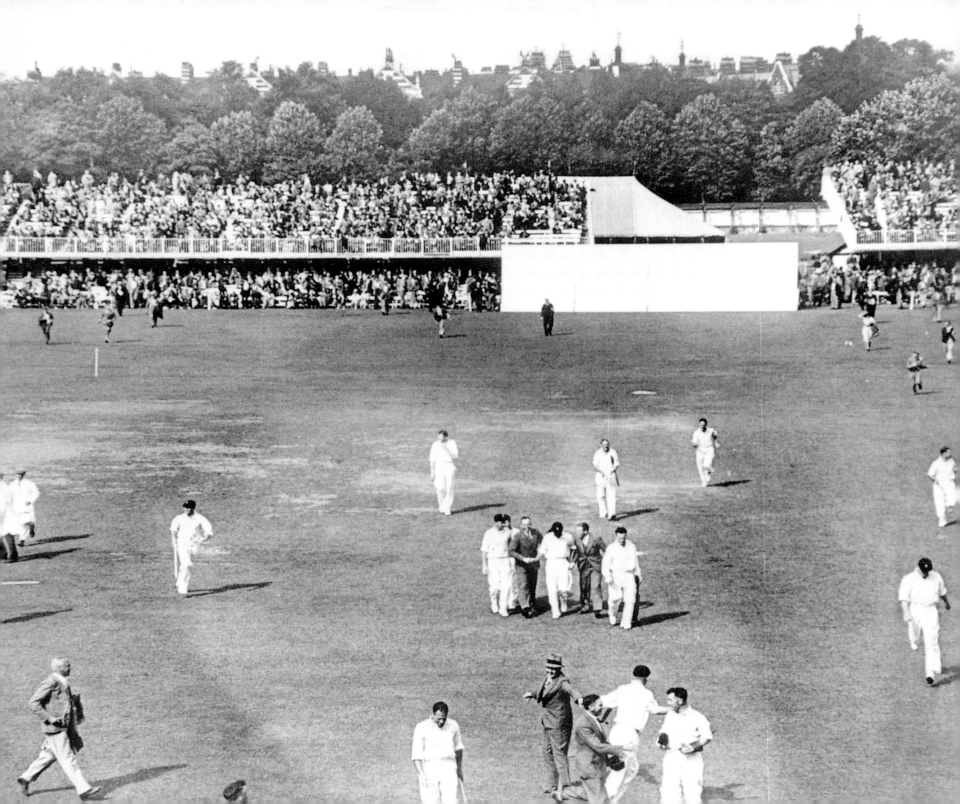

million. The Finance Committee took a deep breath. When it had digested this information, it reported that, without outside assistance, it would not be possible to fund the construction. MCC's great benefactor, John Paul Getty, again came to the rescue. Prompted by his friend Gubby Allen, he promised a sum of £1.6 million, and this enabled the Finance Committee to give the project a green light. The Test and County Cricket Board was also able to help, through its seat scheme, under which the revenue from additional seats created and bought for major matches can be kept by MCC until the cost of those seats has been recovered.

At the end of 1988 the main Committee approved the project, and the architect put in a planning application. Westminster City Council planners liked the proposed scheme, and approved it in February 1989. At an Extraordinary General Meeting the same month the members gave their approval, and the Working Party then started looking for suitable firms to tender for the fixed-price contract,

At this point, however, the Working Party was pressured into

making a significant mistake. The professional team had put forward the names of contractors who they thought had the necessary skills and experience to build a quite complicated engineering structure. Unfortunately, as it turned out, a past member of the Estates Sub-Committee made strong representations on behalf of a particular contractor, John Lelliot Ltd. Although the professional team had not put Lelliot forward, it was, nevertheless, decided to include the firm on the list.

At this time, David Male was appointed President of the Royal Institute of Chartered Surveyors – a position that is not merely honorary, but carries with it considerable responsibilities and obligations, requiring a substantial amount of the incumbent's time. Thus it became necessary for Male to ask Brian Thornton to take over as Chairman of the Working Party.

In July 1989, when the tenders came in, Thornton was faced with his first problem: the lowest tender was for £4.9 million – £1.15 million, or twenty-three per cent, above the budget figure. Apart from the embarrassment such a large difference caused, it meant that a great cost-saving exercise had to be undertaken, to bring the contract sum nearer the budget figure. The programme envisaged a start being made on site at the end of the 1989 season. The time for construction work was very short, because the Club wanted the job to be completed during the close season of 1989–90. In this way, it was assumed, there would be no disruption of play or loss of revenue from seats caused by the works. Thus the cost-saving exercise had to be undertaken under the severest time pressure. After much negotiating, Lelliot was given the go-ahead and demolition of the old G and H stands began on time on 12 September.

Having cleared this first hurdle, the organisers were soon confronted by another: in October the contractor reported that

Demolition of G and H stands began in September 1989.

Contractor's men watching the cricket over the screens, when they were supposed to be working all-out to complete the stands.

Top: Denis Compton opens the Compton and Edrich Stands in June 1991 watched by MCC Secretary Colonel John Stephenson (centre), and Justin Edrich, son of Bill Edrich.

Middle: The clean sweep of the Compton and Edrich Stands seen from the promenade deck of the Mound Stand.

Bottom: The headroom in the Edrich Stand is much improved. Spectators on the lower terrace are now able to see a high ball with few columns to obstruct their view.

Opposite page: The stands full to capacity for the 1991 Test match.

there was going to be a four-week delay in the delivery of the structural steel. Then, just before Christmas, Ove Arup & Partners discovered there had been a mistake in their calculation of the amount of steel needed in the reinforced concrete.

The ramifications of this on both time and cost were considerable, and alarm bells were now ringing. Later some further mistakes were made by the contractor, who, on an engineering project of this complexity, did not seem to have the resources at his disposal to take speedy corrective action. By the end of the year Thornton was in despair and reporting that the stands would not be ready for the start of the 1990 season.

Some might say, 'The rest is history', because the completion of the job was played out in front of all the spectators who came to Lord's through the 1990 season. Attempts were made to screen the works from the ground, but nothing infuriated members more than seeing the men, who were supposed to be toiling flat-out to complete the stands, looking over the screens to watch the cricket. For major matches a temporary stand was erected on the ground in front of the building site.

The stands were eventually completed in March 1991, and at the June Test match they were officially opened by Denis Compton and named the Compton and Edrich Stands. The contractor, who had incurred major additional costs, endeavoured to retrieve some of his losses at the final account stage, but with the assistance of Lord Griffiths, then President of MCC, the Club was able to resist his claims. All parties were left to lick their wounds.

These two stands will probably be remembered more for the disruption they caused than for their aesthetic impact. They are very plain, and although they are a great improvement on their predecessors, some of the seats in the lower terrace of the Compton Stand are still, inevitably, claustrophobic. The quality of

the workmanship is good. The concrete work won a Concrete Society award, and the athletic structural design has given those seated on the lower terraces a much-improved view of the play.

However, in handling this project the Committee had been faced with a dilemma. It had been established, when the new Mound Stand was commissioned, that Lord's should remain a cricket ground of separate pavilions, and should not be turned into a stadium along the lines of Melbourne Cricket Ground.

There was a significant risk that, if the Committee had gone for larger and higher stands, Lord's would have taken on the aspect of a stadium, and also that the view of the trees in the background would have been lost. On the other hand, there is little doubt that, by going for the lower option, an opportunity was lost, not only to increase the capacity of the ground substantially, but also to provide more comfort and shade for spectators on the upper terrace. The dilemma persists: any future development of stands at the Nursery End will inescapably have to consider the over-riding need to maintain the unique character of Lord's as a cricket ground.

Right: The Compton and Edrich Stands seen on completion, with the greatly improved headroom and the preserved view of the trees beyond. This was achieved only by not incorporating a roof and keeping a very plain appearance.

17

The New Indoor School

1993–95

The original indoor cricket school at Lord's, one of the first to be built in England, was completed in 1977. Its existence owed much to the foresight and determination of Jim Swanton and John Haslewood, backed up the generosity of Jack Haywood. It provided seven nets in a building sited behind the Full Toss bar at the Nursery End. Like all the indoor schools that followed its example, the building was entirely enclosed, without windows, so that players were wholly dependent on artificial light. This arrangement was thought to be safest for batsmen, because no shadows or changes in light-level could interfere with the visibility of the ball.

Externally, the structure was a dismal affair, the kind of metal-sided, portal frame-shed that can be seen on any industrial estate, a blot on the horizon when viewed from the Pavilion – or from anywhere else for that matter – and a sad tribute to Jack Hayward's generosity. Inside, it was about as inspiring as a high-bay warehouse. All contact with the outside world was lost; it smelled like an oversized changing-room, and was bathed in stark, glaring fluorescent light. On the other hand, it did provide

A net in progress in the new Indoor School, with no artificial lighting required. The use of natural light has generated significant energy savings.

an artificial 'cricket laboratory' where players of all ages could hone their skills through the dark winter months.

By 1993 the original building was looking very tired and needed considerable expenditure by way of repairs. Informal early indications provided the Committee with good reason to believe that the Foundation for Sport and the Arts might give a grant to cover at least some of the cost of a new building. Thus Dennis Silk, who was President, and the Committee soon came to the conclusion that demolition and the construction of a new indoor school provided the best way forward. David Male, the Chairman of the Estates Sub-Committee, asked Brian Thornton, Peter Bell and John Barclay to join him on a new Working Party to oversee the project.

Their first task was to appoint an architect. Michael Hopkins had done a significant amount of design and research work on sketches which showed possible options for the development of the Nursery End, but the Committee had not in the end favoured these ideas. There was, however, some support in the Working Party for the appointment of Hopkins to design the new school.

The Estates Sub-Committee eventually decided that six practices should be invited to come forward with proposals – Michael Hopkins and Partners, YRM plc, Lobb Partnership, Richard Horden Associates, Building Design Partnership and David Morley Architects. It was largely as a result of a strong recommendation from Peter Bell that David Morley's name was included. The Working Party, with the help of the cricket school management team, set to work preparing a detailed design brief.

In August 1993 each architectural practice presented its proposals. The criteria used for judging the schemes were elegance, function, comfort, durability, ageing and maintenance. Morley produced a design on which, it was clear, a significant amount of research had been lavished, and the Working Party had no difficulty in recommending adoption of his scheme. He was duly appointed in September 1993. Hopkins's scheme was adjudged the runner-up.

Inherent in Morley's innovative design were three significant departures from accepted practice: natural light was to be used to illuminate the nets during the day, while in twilight and dark

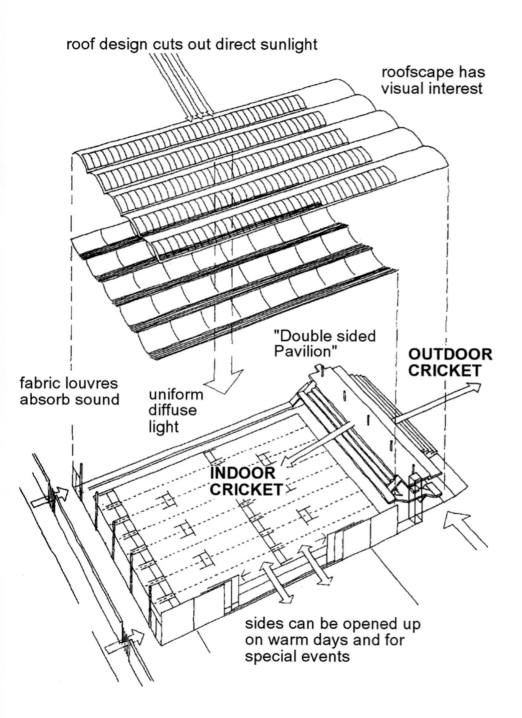

roof design cuts out direct sunlight

roofscape has
visual interest

"Double sided
Pavilion"

**OUTDOOR
CRICKET**

fabric louvres
absorb sound

uniform
diffuse
light

**INDOOR
CRICKET**

sides can be opened up
on warm days and for
special events

hours lighting was to be provided by means of fluorescent tubes running over the length of the nets (in the original school, the tubes had been installed at right angles to the line of the nets). The third change was driven by the other two and involved the design of the roof. Normally, for reasons of economy, the roof loads would be taken by a structure spanning the width of the building. In this case, in order to accommodate the lighting scheme, Nick Hanika of Price & Myers, the structural engineers, produced a design spanning the length of the school.

These changes were a major concern to Gordon Jenkins, manager of the indoor school, and John Stephenson, MCC Secretary, made it clear that they thought the new arrangements might be dangerous for batsmen facing fast bowling. The architect and his specialist services engineer, Max Fordham, gave careful consideration to their concerns and asked for the lighting arrangement to be tested in the old school.

The England batsman Mike Gatting was invited to be the guinea pig and faced some medium-pace bowling in the existing nets, with the lighting rearranged to mimic its proposed new orientation. After a half-hour session, he expressed himself quite happy; the lights had not dazzled him.

The school management remained sceptical about the use of natural light. However, it was decided to test a model of the scheme in an artificial sky laboratory at the Bartlett Institute at University College, London. Eventually, Morley was able to demonstrate to the satisfaction of John Jameson, Gordon Jenkins and Roger Knight (who by then had taken over as Secretary) that his design would be safe and practical and would provide a much more pleasant atmosphere in which to practise.

In February 1994, after the Royal Fine Arts Commission had produced a very positive assessment of the design, Westminster City

One of the drawings submitted by David Morley for the architectural competition, illustrating how the building would function.

Council granted planning consent. By then the estimated construction cost had risen to almost £2 million, and this figure was soon confirmed when Wates Construction Ltd put in a competitive tender. Although the Foundation for Sport and the Arts had yet to confirm its willingness to provide financial assistance, the Committee decided that work must start at the end of the season.

The contract was signed, and work began on site in September 1994, as soon as the Cross Arrows matches were completed.

In October 1994 David Male stepped down as Chairman of the Estates Sub-Committee and Brian Thornton took over this role. However, as Male had taken the lead as Chairman of the Working Party responsible for the new cricket school, Thornton asked him to continue in his role until the project was completed. This he achieved in July 1995, having overcome all the usual tribulations of the building process, on time, within budget and to wide acclaim.

Above: Model used to test the innovative lighting scheme in the artificial sky laboratory at the Bartlett Institute.

Right: The north-light roof structure showing one of the five main trusses.

During construction it was decided that access to the school should be provided from the North Gate, and this meant that a new access road and car park had to be added to the scheme. The opportunity was taken to provide passers-by with a more friendly impression of the new school and ground. A 300-metre-long white-flowering border was installed along the Wellington Road boundary wall, reinforcing the link between the ground and the adjacent public park. This planting was designed by Edward Hutchinson. The loss of a few car-parking spaces generated some criticism from members, but the scheme enhanced the appearance of the approach to the school. To give the school a more outgoing image and to stimulate public interest in its activities, it was also decided that openings should be created in the St John's Wood Road boundary wall to allow glimpses into the school from the pavement.

John Pringle, the partner of Michael Hopkins who had been responsible for the architectural development of the new Mound Stand, assessed the new cricket school in the *RIBA Journal* of October 1995. 'As fellow competitors in the limited competition, our first reaction was critical,' he wrote:

> The roof structure looked a bit contrived. But we had to concede that the solution was ingenious: partly for its plan, but principally for its sophisticated north-light roof. The roof design revolves entirely around the lighting scheme, which is a well-devised reinterpretation of the factory north-light roof, using half-glazed barrel vaults and fabric blinds underneath. This solution overcame all the traditional cricket school objections to natural light, as north light is free from sudden variations caused by the sun. The result is wonderfully light and airy.

A six-a-side match in progress in the new school at night.

An evening match in progress with the side walls open, providing the light and air not found at other indoor schools.

The real triumph is that the new indoor school now feels like a natural extension of the outdoor game, not only because of the daylight, but also because the side walls can open up in summertime to reveal the rest of the ground and let in fresh air. Overall, this building is a great achievement. Morley has succeeded in producing a well thought-out solution, in which planning, structure, services and lighting are locked together in a beautifully integrated design.

The Duke of Edinburgh, accompanied by the President, Sir Oliver Popplewell, opened the new Cricket School on 19 October 1995. A piece to mark the occasion in the October edition of the *RIBA Journal*, written by Geraint John, Chief Architect at the Sports Council of Great Britain, was particularly gratifying:

This building represents the very vision of Britain's new sports facilities, it is exemplary. Morley's building addresses the government's recently published policy statement, 'Sport: raising the game', which aims to raise the status and importance of sport in public life.

What could achieve these aims more successfully than a well-researched training building, which actively fosters the next generation of sporting heroes? Great care has been taken, as with Michael Hopkins' Mound Stand, to set the building skilfully into its context, to provide good quality landscaping and to allow clever glimpses into the building from the exterior – and all has been achieved without compromising the function of the building.

The result is that the building has a distinguished presence: it

Left: The barrel-vaulted north-light roof and the opening side walls, seen from the south.

Centre: The north elevation depicting the entrance, terrace and viewing gallery for spectators of matches on the Nursery Ground.

Right: A match in progress on the Nursery Ground with the new indoor school providing seating for spectators and a much improved backdrop for the game.

is uncompromisingly modern, but yet respectful of its surroundings. It has a refreshing simplicity, which has resulted from the care taken with both the research and the design. But, above all, it is a practical building, which will encourage and enable a spirit of excellence to flourish and will help to stimulate higher standards in sports buildings throughout the United Kingdom.

The new school received several accolades in 1996, including:

- The RIBA Award for Architecture
- The RIBA Architecture in Sport and Leisure Award

- Runner-up for the Stirling Prize
- The Structural Steel Award
- Structural Steel Innovation Award
- Aluminium Imagination Award
- Runner-up *Financial Times* Award

Design Team:
Architects: David Morley Architects
Structural Engineers: Price & Myers
Environmental Services Consultant: Max Fordham & Partners
Cost Consultant: Davis Langdon & Everest
Contractor: Wates Construction

18

The New Grand Stand
1994–98

In May 1994 David Male commissioned two studies to assess the comparative potential benefits of redeveloping either the Grand Stand or the Tavern Stand. Both were in a state of disrepair, and it was important to establish which site would, through renovation, generate the greatest benefit to MCC. Michael Hopkins was asked to study the potential of the Tavern site, while Nicholas Grimshaw investigated the other.

It was clear from their reports that the 1926 Grand Stand offered the greatest potential gain, both in numbers of extra seats and in improved conditions for spectators. In December 1994 Sir Oliver Popplewell, as President, and the Committee decided that Baker's building should be demolished to make way for a new structure. The concrete structure of the old stand was rotting; it had become unpopular with spectators (forty-three per cent of the seats had obstructed views of the playing area); the boxes and dining rooms were not up to modern standards, and it was important that Lord's should have the best possible facilities for the World Cup in 1999. Brian Thornton, the newly-appointed Chairman of the Estates Sub-Committee, was asked for proposals to be placed before the Committee as soon as possible.

A Working Party was quickly assembled consisting of

The high central mast of the new Grand Stand from which the roof is suspended by hangers through the tubular steel prismatic truss.

Thornton as Chairman, Peter Bell, John Gasson, David Male and James Offen, with Roger Knight, Secretary, and John Smith, Assistant Secretary (Administration) completing the team on behalf of the Executive. The first matter to consider was the appointment of an architect. The Estates Sub-Committee was split on the issue, the majority being in favour of holding a competition. But Thornton and a minority of the Sub-Committee were concerned about the shortage of time. They pointed out that this, combined with the sensitivity of the site and the proposed demolition of a building by a well-known architect, made the appointment of Nicholas Grimshaw, who had already done the initial study, the better way forward. The Main Committee agreed and Grimshaw was appointed in March 1995.

Until then, major building projects at Lord's had been managed by a duo consisting of the Assistant Secretary (Administration) and the Chairman of the Working Party. It was decided that a scheme as large and complex as that for the new Grand Stand required the skills of a professional Project Manager, who would be responsible for day-to-day running. Selection interviews were held in March 1995 to find the most suitable people to fill this role. Gardiner & Theobald Management Services were appointed, with Simon Jones and Guy Macaulay the individuals concerned. Both were instrumental in achieving the successful outcome of the project.

The rest of the design team were soon appointed. John Thornton of Ove Arup & Partners, who had worked as structural engineer on the Mound Stand and also with Nicholas Grimshaw on several of his projects, was given this role. Richard Baldwin of Davis Langdon & Everest, who had worked for MCC on the Mound Stand, was appointed quantity surveyor, making up, with the others, the core of the design team.

The Working Party prepared a brief which stated that the construction of the new stand was to be phased over two close-seasons. This meant that all the work on site had to be undertaken during the winters of 1996–97 and 1997–98, with completion of the first phase providing public seating for the 1997 season, and final completion ready for the 1998 season. Clearly this was a demanding programme, but the Committee wanted to be sure that any teething problems, which were likely to be experienced in a project of this complexity, would be resolved before the World Cup scheduled for 1999.

Nicholas Grimshaw decided the only possible way of meeting the deadlines was to design a building whose major elements could be prefabricated off-site. He proposed that large parts of the new stand could be manufactured during the summer months, when no work was permitted on-site, and then fixed in position at Lord's during the winter. This strategy was soon agreed, and became fundamental to the design.

In Grimshaw's office David Harriss and David Portman worked all-out to produce their studies by May 1995. Their ideas were impressive, but they made it clear that the first major hurdle was going to be obtaining planning permission. There were rumours that the old Baker Grand Stand would be listed, and some owners of adjoining properties outside the ground were beginning to voice concerns about its demolition. The Committee therefore decided to appoint consultants on difficult planning and rights-of-light/party-wall issues. Hugh Bullock of chartered surveyors Gerald Eve was brought on to the planning roll, while Lance Harris of Anstey Horne & Company gave valuable advice on MCC's position under the rights-of-light/party-wall law. He was also able to advise on the rights enjoyed by the neighbours as far as sunlight and daylight were concerned.

Over the next few months discussions took place with Westminster City Council planners; meetings were held at Permanent Secretary level at the Department of the Environment and with the Chairman of English Heritage. By August English Heritage had decided that the Baker Grand Stand was 'neither listable nor within the curtilage of the Pavilion.' Although these decisions removed a major hurdle, many other considerations of planning, rights-of-light and boundary rights meant that significant changes were required to the initial designs. In September all the immediate neighbours were invited to Lord's to view the drawings and model. Soon afterwards a press conference was held to give the public an understanding of MCC's intentions. This was a prelude to the actual submission of the planning application, which was placed with Westminster City Council on 12 September 1995.

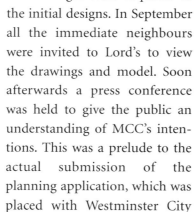

Roger Knight and Brian Thornton show a model of the new stand to the Press, with the old Baker Grand Stand in the background. At this stage it was envisaged that a new scoreboard would be located in the centre of the new stand, with the Old Father Time weather vane on the roof above.

Later presentations were made to representatives of the Royal Fine Arts Commission, English Heritage, the St John's Wood Society and finally to members of the Planning Committee of Westminster City Council. Without exception their responses were positive, but some of the neighbours, whose gardens lay next to the north side of the ground, naturally remained worried. In particular the owner of 29 Cavendish Close, Martin Boston, said he would do all he could to resist the granting of planning permission. However, it seemed that the architectural press would support MCC. For example, writing in the *Independent* on 9 December, Jim White stated: 'The MCC, this apparent bastion of all that is fuddy and duddy, has developed into the most energetic patron of modern architecture in Britain.'

On 28 March 1996 planning permission was granted to demolish the Baker Grand Stand and to construct Grimshaw's new Grand Stand, with its 6,200 seats and twenty boxes. The original design envisaged a new scoreboard in the centre of the building at box level, replicating the location of its predecessor. It also showed the Old Father Time weather vane fixed at high level above the roof. Brian Thornton had expressed some reservations about both these features, but it was decided to allow planning permission to be granted on the basis of the original scheme and to ask, if necessary, for it to be changed at a later date.

At the Annual General Meeting of MCC, which took place on 1 May 1996, Walter Garretts, one of the members, pointed out the benefits of locating scoreboards on the diagonal axis of cricket grounds. He asked why a new scoreboard was proposed in the very centre of the new stand, where it would occupy the space of several boxes and seats in prime positions. In fact it had been proving extremely difficult to display all the information required in the confined space available in the position originally chosen, and after Garretts' intervention, the Working Party decided that the scoreboard should be relocated over the Compton Stand. Since the Committee had just received planning permission for the new stand with the scoreboard at its centre, this proved an awkward decision to implement.

For the construction of the stand, Richard Baldwin had recommended the adoption of a management form of contract, and in July 1996, after an exhaustive selection process, Heery International Ltd were appointed to start their pre-contract work. Neil Pailing was to be the project manager on site and Mike Grice the director in charge. Soon they became closely involved with Martin Boston, the owner of 29 Cavendish Close, concerning the demolition of the old stand.

On 29 August 1996 a Special General Meeting was called at which members were asked to approve the project. Despite the fact that the stand now had an overall cost-tag of £13 million, and the Sports Council had decided, in principle, to refuse a Lottery Grant, there was a substantial majority in favour of proceeding. (The Sports Council had turned down the Lottery application because the Club rules excluded women from membership, and also because the new stand was not a facility to be used by participating sportsmen and women.) The Finance Committee, under the Chairmanship of David Hudd, reported that a combination of the ECB seat scheme and the sale of boxes and debenture seats, would allow MCC to repay the bank loan, required to fund the project, within ten years of completion. This, and the skilful handling of the meeting by the President, was enough to convince members.

The demolition of the old Baker stand started on 15 September 1996, the day after the last match of the season. Although a tricky process, which had to be carried out with great care in order not to disturb or damage neighbouring properties, the work went well. Old Father Time was taken down and removed to a workshop for refurbishment. There were long and difficult nego-

The model of the new stand, showing the four aerofoil wing roof panels held in position by two fifty-metre-long tubular steel trusses, and the retractable blinds that provide shade for the debenture seating below.

The lower terrace of the new stand in use in the 1997 season. Accommodating 4,200 spectators, it had a new scoreboard mounted on the central column which would carry the superstructure that was being prefabricated while the cricket season was in progress.

tiations with Martin Boston's solicitors, which even involved a visit to the High Court in November to obtain a ruling about the ownership of the boundary wall, before it could be taken down. There was also an argument about a couple of bricks which came to be lying on the lawn of 29 Cavendish Close. Nevertheless, the foundations of the new stand went in on time in December. This was good news for the Working Party; but even better news came in March 1997, when they learned that, in a quite different

context, Martin Boston and his brother had been found guilty of conspiracy to pervert the course of justice and had been sentenced to two years' imprisonment.

The lower terrace of the new stand was completed by April 1997 with 4,200 new seats in position. Catering facilities and new toilets were provided in the undercroft. Almost a year earlier, in May 1996, David Morley had been appointed to obtain planning permission for a scoreboard over the Compton Stand. In an extraordinary decision, Westminster City Council had refused permission. It was therefore decided to launch an appeal, but it was not until June 1997 that the inspector found in MCC's favour and upheld the appeal. In the meantime the Working Party had taken the risk of ordering the new scoreboard, so that it could be used in a temporary position at the back of the new terrace for the 1997 season. Old Father Time was returned to Lord's in time for the first match of the season, but he had to be located in a temporary position above the Mound Stand clock tower. He has remained there since, because it was feared he would be out of proportion with the magnitude of the new Grand Stand roof and mast.

Throughout the summer of 1997, while cricket was being played on the ground, work progressed with the fabrication of the steel truss and girders at Watson Steel in Bolton and the pre-cast concrete units at Tarmac's factory in Tallington near Stamford.

Pre-cast concrete coffered floor unit, cast in white cement at Tallington in Lincolnshire. Weighing 20 tonnes, each of these twenty-eight units formed the floor of a box. The underside formed the ceiling above the spectators seated on the lower terrace.

The Old Father Time weather vane in its 'temporary' location atop the Mound Stand clock tower. It remains in this position today and will probably do so unless or until a more suitable site is found.

These massive elements would be assembled on site and form the superstructure of the new stand. Work on site began again in September. The new seats and scoreboard were removed and the construction process re-started. Two large cranes were stationed on the outfield, with a temporary road that led across the Nursery Ground, through the gap between the Compton and Edrich stands and on across the outfield. Delivery of the steel truss and pre-cast concrete units required police escorts through the streets of London at night. At the ground, the cranes lifted the sections of the truss into position: each one, weighing 62 tonnes, had to be placed with the greatest care to ensure the very tight tolerances were achieved, so that each element could be fitted together perfectly. The superstructure is not so much a building as a bridge, supported by just three columns and the spine beam or truss, which is two storeys high.

Planning permission was now required to remove the scoreboard from the new Grand Stand. The implications of its removal on the structure of the building were quite significant. By the time the appeal against the refusal of permission for the Compton Stand scoreboard was upheld, the contractors were well ahead with the manufacture of the structural elements of this part of the stand. It was therefore necessary for two sets of parts to be prefabricated: one for the stand as originally conceived, and the second without the scoreboard. This was the only way of ensuring that the structure would be completed on time, while the weeks went by and Westminster City Council went through its planning procedure. At last, in August 1997, permission was granted, and the stand in its final configuration could be completed.

Neil Pailing and his team were up against a very demanding time schedule for completion by May 1998, and they also had to manage the extremely complex assembly of the different elements. For example, the entire superstructure was built up on a cradle of temporary works. It was only when the whole assembly was complete that de-propping could start and the 3,000-tonne structure could be lowered onto the spine beam. This was done by eighty-two 90-tonne jacks working together and controlled, over a period of three weeks, by one central computer. The construction team rose to this and the many other challenges with which they were presented, and completed the new Grand Stand, ready for the 1998 season, within the £13 million budget.

Commenting on his new creation, Nicholas Grimshaw said:

> The effect of the all-white stand on a summer day is almost ethereal. Despite its size, it has a delicacy which renders it neutral; it does not detract from the action on the pitch one iota. When seen in actuality, its articulated presence is much more powerful and its relationship to the other buildings around the ground becomes clear. These are summer pavilions, with something of a temporary encampment about them. For all its permanence as a structure, you could almost imagine the Grand Stand being packed up and taken away as the season ends and the evenings draw in.

The Duke of Edinburgh, accompanied by the President, opened the stand on 18 June 1998, ready for the first Test match of the season against South Africa. The ground was packed with spectators eager to see the South Africans on tour for the first time since 1985, and although the opening day produced numerous teething problems, such as a complete power failure, everybody who had contributed to the new building was greatly heartened by comments made by spectators in the public seats

The 100-metre-long lower terrace with the superstructure above, carried on just three columns. Its simplicity belies a complex structure of differing elements. It is really bridge engineering, with very large scale members running through occupied spaces.

Right: Having cut the ribbon to open the stand, the Duke of Edinburgh hands the scissors to Colin Ingleby-Mackenzie, President.

Opposite page: The new Grand Stand in all its splendour.

Elaine Knutt reported in *Building* magazine on 29 May 1998: 'The completed stand is a triumph of structural engineering, millimetre-accurate prefabrication and innovation. The 100-metre length of the upper level is supported on just three columns, creating the illusion of floating.'

John Pringle writing in the *Architects' Journal* on 27 August 1998, agreed: 'The new Grand Stand at Lord's echoes the transport metaphors of other recent additions to "England's biggest village cricket ground" to produce a spectacular celebration of technical prowess.' Alan Lee in *The Times* wrote: 'The new Grand Stand is a triumph, in the views it affords, the comfort of the seating and the ribbon of bars and catering outlets at ground level.'

and boxes, and also by the positive reaction of the media.

'Even the mizzle of a grey London morning could not deny the splendour of the new stand,' wrote Michael Henderson in *The Times* on 19 June 1998. 'As the millennium approaches, Lord's is transforming itself into a ground, stadium if you prefer, with a future as glorious as its past.'

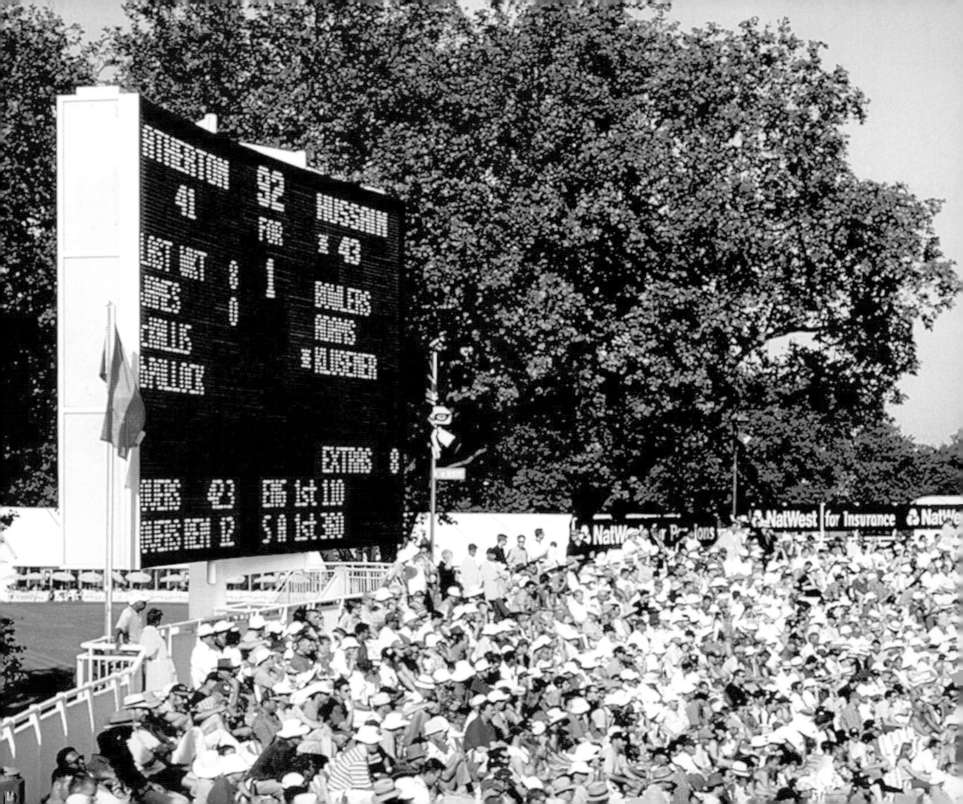

19

New Scoreboards

1996–98

Until 1997 Lord's had two scoreboards, mounted on either side of the ground at right-angles to the wicket. One was to the north, high up in the centre of the Baker Grand Stand, and the other to the south, between the Tavern and Mound Stands. The Grand Stand board functioned in the traditional telegraph manner, with operators changing the figures by hand whenever the score moved. The scorers were housed in a room behind the face of the board, with a window looking out over the ground. Operators and scorers were in continuous communication, to ensure that information was displayed correctly.

The board on the south side of the ground had been installed after the completion of the new Mound Stand in 1987. It replaced the hand-operated telegraph box that had been in place since 1950, and it was the first electronically-controlled scoreboard to be used at Lord's – but it was never entirely satisfactory, being difficult to read and often faulty.

It was at the AGM in 1996 that a member, Walter Garretts, pointed out to the Committee how inappropriate were the locations of the scoreboards. He suggested that, before compounding the error by placing a new one in the new Grand Stand, thought should be given to setting both boards on the

north-east/south-west diagonal axis. Much work had been done on the design of the latest electronic display, for which planning permission had been obtained, but it was proving very difficult to accommodate all the necessary information within the space available. The ever-growing scoreboard was, in fact, beginning to take up valuable space in the new stand, causing the removal of boxes and debenture seats.

The scoreboard mounted in the Baker Stand which was in use until the end of the 1996 season.

The Compton Stand scoreboard showing how its curved face provides legible information even when viewed from an acute angle.

Top: The first remotely controlled scoreboard to be used at Lord's, installed in 1988 between the Mound Stand and the Tavern Stand.

Centre: This model of the new Grand Stand shows how a new scoreboard would have looked mounted at its centre. This scheme did not proceed. The scoreboard was eventually mounted above the Compton Stand.

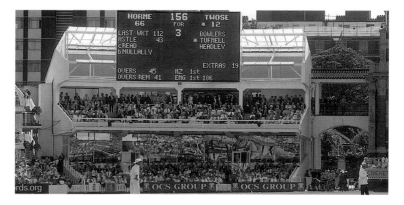

Bottom: The roof of the Allen Stand was altered in order to accommodate the second scoreboard on the transverse axis of the ground.

Thus it was with some relief that Brian Thornton seized upon Mr Garretts' suggestion. Little did he know how difficult implementation of the change would prove to be.

It was decided to take the proposed electronic board out of the new Grand Stand and mount it high up over the Compton Stand. In May 1996 David Morley was instructed to prepare a design and obtain planning permission. He went to work quickly, and with the help of Ove Arup & Partners soon produced a most elegant structure to support the new board.

Planning permission was applied for in September 1996, and, three months later, to the consternation of the Working Party, was refused on the casting vote of the Chairman of the Planning Committee of Westminster City Council. The Council had already taken until December to make up their minds, and there was not much time to change the design of the new Grand Stand, to reflect the possible removal of the scoreboard.

MCC's decision to appeal against the refusal was a quick and easy one. Robert Griffiths, QC, a planning counsel and member of the Estates Committee, gave valuable support in the preparation of written evidence. Although the inspector took only two weeks to deliver his verdict, it was not until June 1997 that the appeal was upheld and work on the new structure could start again.

While the planning situation was being clarified, manufacture of the board itself had gone ahead in Atlanta, Georgia. It was shipped over to England and used during the 1997 season, mounted in a temporary position at the back of the new Grand Stand terrace. Thus, all those seated on the south side of the ground benefited from the clear and concise information it provided. The scorers, having lost their position behind the old Grand Stand board, were now housed in a temporary box at the top of the Warner Stand. The new board is worked by computers, and the operators sit alongside the scorers to make sure that the information displayed is always accurate.

Work on the foundation behind the Compton Stand, which would carry the structure for the board, started in September 1997. This was a tricky process because it was so close to the new Grand Stand works, which were proceeding flat-out at the same time. However, everything was ready for the 1998 season and the elegant new Compton Stand scoreboard has been operating to everyone's satisfaction since then.

As soon as the electronic board came into use, even in its temporary position, the shortcomings of the Mound Stand were painfully obvious. It had also become unreliable, and because the ground would soon have a new board over the Compton Stand and the other between the Mound and Tavern Stands, many spectators in the Compton and Edrich Stands would not be able to see any scoreboard at all.

Thornton had had his eye on the roof of the Allen Stand as the most promising site for a second diagonal-axis board, and he soon obtained the approval of the Committee to go ahead with an initial study. In December 1997 David Morley was instructed to prepare a feasibility study; by July 1998 the proposed alterations had been approved by the Working Party and planning permission was granted in August. Great care was taken to ensure that the orientation of the new scoreboard would allow as many spectators in the Warner Stand as possible to be able to see the information displayed (there are still a few seats in this stand that do not have a clear view of a scoreboard). Installation work started in September and proceeded according to plan, until the new scoreboard was connected up ready for the start of the World Cup season.

The members who sit in the Allen Stand received the changes

An artist's impression of the Warner Stand illustrating how it would appear if the changes envisaged to accommodate a replay screen were implemented.

to the roof with acclamation. The alterations have not only improved the appearance of the stand, which, beforehand, could only be described as 'agricultural', but they have also given a much brighter environment in which the spectators can watch the cricket. Lord's now provides one of the best and clearest scoreboard information services to spectators anywhere in the country.

The board between the Mound and Tavern stands has now been removed to make way for a new scorers' box, in a position that will replicate the site the scorers enjoyed in the old Grand Stand. For major matches a replay screen is erected over the Edrich Stand, but only about two-thirds of the spectators can see it. To remedy this deficiency, it will be necessary to mount a second screen in the roof of the Warner Stand. David Morley has prepared a scheme which provides a most elegant solution: his design was chosen as the best of four submitted to MCC. As yet funds are not available to implement the scheme, but there is little doubt that it will not only enhance the appearance of the stand, but also create better facilities for members and give every spectator complete coverage of replays.

20

England and Wales Cricket Board Headquarters, Lord's Shop and the Nursery Pavilion

1994–99

For nearly ten years from 1982 the Test and County Cricket Board was accommodated in purpose-built offices at Lord's; but by 1991 it had become clear that they needed much more space. The Committee, with Lord Griffiths as President, was also concerned about the offices for the MCC's own staff, who worked in the Dickensian conditions of the Pavilion's basement. The only practical solution was to build new offices for the TCCB and move the MCC staff into the premises which the Board vacated.

With the Compton and Edrich stands being completed, and the new Cricket School in the design stage, there was considerable building activity at the time. Thus it was not until December 1994, when Sir Oliver Popplewell was President, that David Morley was commissioned to design the new office building. Brian Thornton

Left: The new ECB Headquarters beside the new Indoor School form the back-drop for a match on the Nursery Ground.

Opposite page: One of the three main halls in the Nursery Pavilion ready to serve lunch to debenture holders from the new Grand Stand.

kept the Working Party, which was in charge of the new Cricket School, in place to oversee the TCCB offices. He chaired the Working Party and soon agreed with his colleagues that Morley should be commissioned to design the new offices.

The chosen site was sandwiched between the new Cricket School and Michael Hopkins's much-praised Mound Stand. Morley had managed to design an indoor school that held its own in the shadow of a building consistently cited as one of the best of its decade, and the Working Party decided to build on that success.

The brief asked for 12,000 square feet of energy-efficient office space in a building that would be as flexible in use as possible. There was also a requirement for possible future access underneath it, from St John's Wood Road to the site of the original cricket school, which had been demolished.

The solution was an unusual combination of vertical steel columns and horizontal concrete floor slabs, chosen on both aesthetic and environmental grounds. The concrete provides the necessary thermal mass for cooling, whereas the slender, circular, hollow-section steel columns give the façade a smooth finish and minimise the amount of light blocked out by their width.

Light shelves were designed to run the length of the building on the first and second floors, cantilevered off the steel columns: these throw the sun's rays up across the ceiling and deep into the floor plan, which is 15.3 metres across. The arrangement creates a naturally-lit environment throughout the day and limits the need for artificial lighting. An aluminium grille platform is fitted into the gap between the reflectors and the windows in order to provide easy access for cleaning and maintenance. The long elevations are glazed from desktop height to ceiling, allowing uninterrupted views through the open-plan office area.

The planning application was submitted in January 1995, and permission was granted in time for tenders to be considered in June. Tolent Construction submitted the lowest tender, which was accepted, so that work could start on site in September 1995, at the end of the cricket season. The contract went very much according to plan: the 12,000 square feet of space were completed on time in June 1996, and within the budget of £1.4 million.

Lord's Shop

Soon after site-work on the new offices had begun, the Committee turned its attention to the MCC's shop, located in a cottage near the East Gate. The Finance Committee had recommended action to improve the shop's poor performance, and the Estates Sub-Committee, of which Sir Ian MacLaurin was a

Left: The sun shelves fitted at first and second floors throw light into the building and provide access for cleaning the windows.

Right: Slender, round hollow section steel columns provide a smooth finish to the façade and minimise the amount of light blocked out by their width.

Left: The East Gate Lodge which housed the shop until 1996.

Right: The entrance to the new shop, and the inflatable foils of the roof which provide natural light within.

member, recommended demolition and the provision of temporary selling-space in portakabins. It was late in the year to be considering such a move if the portakabins were to be ready for the start of the 1996 season. However, Brian Thornton and David Male were reasonably confident it could be done. The Committee, with Sir Oliver Popplewell at the helm, gave the go-ahead.

Because Lord's is in a conservation area, planning permission was required to demolish the old cottage that housed the shop. The idea of temporary portakabins soon had to be discarded, when it became clear that permission would not be forthcoming unless the replacement building preserved and enhanced the character of the conservation area.

In 1995 David Morley was appointed to come up with a low-cost design which would provide the retail space required and also satisfy the planners. With the discreet assistance of some Tesco personnel, he designed the shop to draw people's gaze in towards the Lord's merchandise. A clear, double-glazed entrance screen would be effective in attracting the attention of passers-by, and the translucent roof, formed with inflatable 'foils' or cushions, combined a high level of insulation and sufficient natural light to obviate the need for artificial illumination.

Morley submitted the planning application in December, obtained tenders in January 1996, and appointed Tolent Construction to carry out the works in March 1996. The job was completed in just eleven weeks and the shop opened in May, ready for the first major match of the season. It cost £200,000 and provided the Club with 3,000 square feet of retail space. In the first year of trading the net revenue to the Club doubled, and it is now about four times the original figure.

Morley treated the roofs of both buildings as 'fourth elevations', being aware that they were overlooked by the tall residential blocks along St John's Wood Road. The TCCB headquarters' roof

Left: A busy day at the new shop.

Right: The ECB Headquarters, completed in June 1996.

was landscaped with gravel and plant boxes, while the shop's translucent roof has a light, white appearance in keeping with the Lord's style. By night the strip lighting glows through the roof like skeletal ribs.

In style, both buildings are complementary not only to Hopkins' Mound Stand, but also to Morley's Cricket School. By going for a low-key, calm design the architect cleverly achieved a hierarchy among the close family of disparate buildings. But the buildings are by no means dull. Like some beautifully-designed Italian dress, they are eye-catching, rather striking and without frippery.

The Nursery Pavilion

As the demand grew for corporate hospitality facilities at Lord's, so the number of marquees increased to meet the need.

Permission to erect these temporary structures had had to be obtained from Westminster City Council each year, and in 1996 the Planning Authority began to complain about the proliferation of tents that remained in place at Lord's throughout the summer.

There was also a looming problem of where the debenture holders in the top tier of the new Grand Stand were going to be provided with refreshments. The restaurant on the floor below their seats was going to be capable of accommodating only about two hundred people.

After several attempts to find a prefabricated temporary building large enough to cope with up to 1,000 people sitting down to lunch, Brian Thornton decided that none of the proposals would satisfy either the Estates Committee or Westminster City Council. Yet another Working Party was assembled, and in September 1997 David Morley was invited to produce a design that would provide dining facilities for

Designed to replace the many marquees that were erected before and then taken down after each match, this elegant building spans the railway tunnels below with foundations and drainage no more than 450mm deep.

debenture holders, and also a flexible space for banqueting, training and exhibitions.

The only site available for a building of such a size was the car-parking area along the Wellington Road side of the Nursery Ground. The railway tunnels that run under the site are only a few metres below the surface, and thus the load that can be imposed on them is severely restricted, and had to be agreed by Railtrack's engineers.

Morley's design overcame these constraints and met the brief in a most elegant manner. The building was to be built directly off the surface of the car park, with no floor slab. The floor was to follow the natural slope of the ground and have no steps in it. With the structural engineers, Atelier One, Morley devised a lightweight steel framework to support two independent struc-

tural membranes, which formed the white tented roof. Basically the building was to be a temporary structure that could be moved to an alternative location when it had fulfilled its purpose. The simplicity of Morley's solution, while echoing the tented roof of the Mound Stand, reinforced the 'village green' character of the Nursery Ground.

Planning permission was granted in time for tenders to be obtained in April 1998. The contract was let for £1.6 million, with work starting in September, and the building was completed in April 1999, just in time for the start of the World Cup season. The overall effect is low-key in relation to the ground's principal buildings, but provides 10,500 square feet of useful floor space for the many and disparate functions held at Lord's in summer and winter.

21

The NatWest
Media Centre

1995–99

At the Main Committee meeting in April 1995 the President, Sir Oliver Popplewell, invited David Richards, Chief Executive of the International Cricket Council, to inform members about the facilities that cricket grounds staging World Cup matches would be expected to provide for the international media. It was made clear that arrangements at Lord's, in particular for the press, were woefully inadequate. The ground, where it was hoped the final would be played, had to be able to accommodate at least 200 journalists and a multitude of television and radio commentators.

Tony Lewis, a member of the Committee with considerable experience in television broadcasting, agreed that new facilities were essential. If Lord's was to remain the world's premier cricket ground, it had to have first-class facilities for both broadcast commentary and written reports. He recommended that any new media centre should therefore be sited behind the bowler's arm. The Committee accepted his suggestion, and Brian Thornton was asked to come forward with proposals for a building that met this brief and would be ready for the start of the World Cup in 1999.

A Working Party was selected from members of the Estates

The curved structure of the Media Centre belies its actual size. To accommodate all the people that work in it and their facilities in a conventional structure would have required a building that appeared much larger.

Sub-Committee consisting of John Gasson, Peter Bell, John Josling and Brian Thornton as Chairman. Roger Knight, Chris Rea, Tony Fleming and John Smith represented the executive.

The selection of a site was simple. Of the two locations available, the only practical possibility was behind the bowler's arm at the Nursery End, the Pavilion end being impractical for reasons of sight-line and town planning. To choose an architect, the Working Party decided to hold a limited competition, with four practices invited to participate. These were GMW, Lifschutz-Davidson, David Morley and Future Systems. The last was included, at Peter Bell's request, as the wild card. Few of the buildings designed by Future Systems had actually been constructed; on the other hand the firm had a high reputation in the profession and had been involved in a design exercise for the MCC, investigating the practicality of a transparent sight-screen.

The four designs, submitted in May 1995, were judged by the Estates Sub-Committee, with Tony Lewis in attendance. The

Working Party decided that the David Morley and Future Systems proposals were the most exciting, and should be taken further in design development before a final selection was made. This was accepted by the Estates Sub-Committee, even though the two schemes were very different, both in appearance and cost.

Each architect was then asked to produce a second option, excluding the accommodation for journalists. After these had been costed, the Estates Sub-Committee met again, but was divided, with a small majority in favour of the Morley solution. Brian Thornton and Tony Lewis were in favour of the Future Systems proposal, with backing from Peter Bell and John Josling. It was decided to present both schemes to the Committee, leaving it to make the final selection.

The Committee met in November 1995, and after Thornton had made his presentation, with a strong recommendation for the Future Systems scheme, the President called for a vote, having made it plain that he himself, the Treasurer, Michael Melluish,

Right: Lifschutz-Davidson's competition drawing for the Media Centre (left), and David Morley's (right).

Opposite page: One of Future Systems' winning submission drawings.

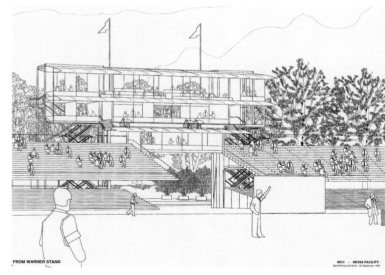

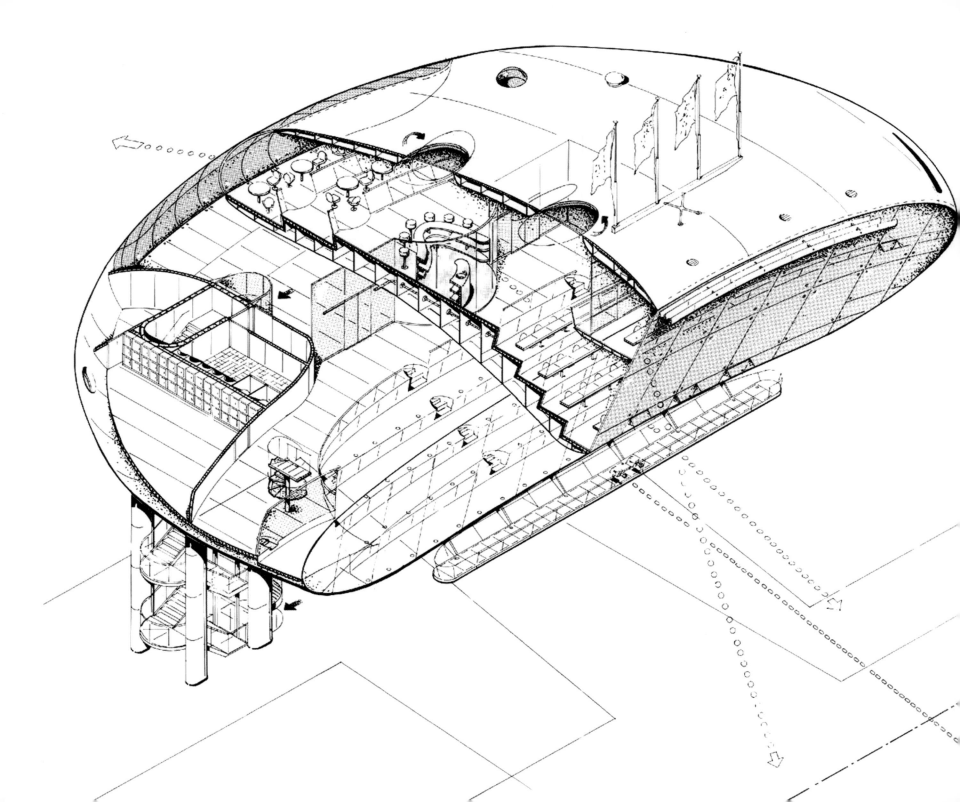

Left: A structural diagram generated by the structural engineers' computer software.

Right: The model being tested in the artificial sky laboratory.

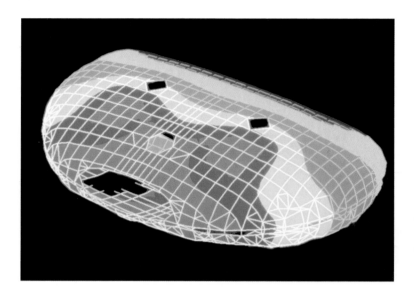

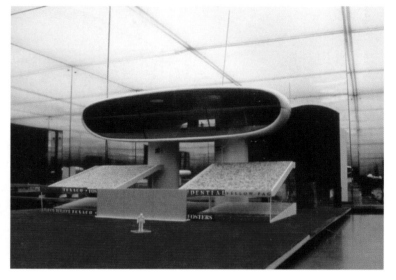

and the Secretary, Roger Knight, were in favour of the Morley Scheme. All the other members voted for the Future Systems design, despite the very large difference in the projected cost: Morley's scheme had been estimated to cost £1.9 million, while the Future Systems scheme was estimated at £2.7 million.

Future Systems was a small practice. Jan Kaplicky and his wife, Amanda Levete, had very little assistance in their office, and were soon under pressure to produce information for the structural engineers, Ove Arup & Partners, and the quantity surveyors, Davis Langdon & Everest. David Miller was recruited from another practice as project architect.

One of the first changes the designers were asked to make was to enlarge the building in order to provide two boxes for use by a potential sponsor. Kaplicky and Levete worked closely with David Glover, the structural engineer in charge at Ove Arup, to produce a shape that could accommodate the extra space. Meanwhile

negotiations began with the NatWest Bank with a view to securing their sponsorship.

Simon Jones and Guy Macaulay from Gardiner and Theobald Management Services were given responsibility for managing the design team and producing a programme of work that would complete the building in time for the World Cup. It was also decided that Hugh Bullock of Gerald Eve would be appointed to advise on the strategy for obtaining planning consent. The glass wall of the new building, overlooking the ground, was another element that needed specialist skills, and these were provided by Sean Billings of Billings Design Associates.

With the full team in place, work began on the preparation of the drawings and other information required to obtain planning permission. The strategy adopted was to develop the design to a very detailed level and then submit it. This would give little room for manoeuvre if the planners did not like what they saw, but MCC was keen not to have changes imposed on the shape of the building.

In September 1996, before the planning application went in, a press conference was held at Lord's to inform the media and public at large about the project. With one or two notable exceptions the response was positive, and the conference evoked headlines such as 'Time For A Leap of Faith' (*The Times*) and 'MCC Expected To Beam Up Media To Space Age' (*Daily Telegraph*). The *Telegraph* also announced that 'the monocoque design for the Media Centre at Lord's has put the wind up the traditionalists – but not in the Pavilion'.

The strategy worked. Westminster City Council planners loved the design, as did the Royal Fine Arts Commission, and even English Heritage gave their approval, despite some misgivings about the impact on views from Regent's Park. In November 1996 planning permission was granted, with the condition that the existing commentary boxes in the turrets of the Pavilion were removed and the turrets returned to their original use as additional viewing areas for members.

During the intervening period a great deal of work had been undertaken on development of the design. Roger Knight and John Jameson, the Head of Cricket, had expressed concern that batsmen might be distracted by movement within the building, and that reflections off the glass wall might distract both the batsmen and fielders. A model of the building was made and tests were carried out at Bartlett University College in London in order to confirm that there would not be any problems.

It was decided that the construction work would be let under two building contracts, the first for the construction of the reinforced concrete pylons which support the superstructure and contain the access stairs and lifts. This contract was awarded to Heery International, who were already building the new Grand Stand nearby.

The second contract covered the construction of the aluminium shell and the installation of internal services and finishings. But before any building work could begin, the approval of the members was required. The first step was to hold an informal meeting in the Long Room on 28 October 1996. Having seen the Press reports and heard that the Royal Fine Art Commission had given its wholehearted support to the project, the 150 members who attended expressed differing views about the design. Lord Palumbo, Chairman of the Arts Council, was effusive in his praise, and imbued the meeting with a very positive atmosphere.

With planning permission granted and a good response from members, it was time to obtain the formal consent of the membership at a Special General Meeting, called for 16 December 1996. The meeting was held in the Banqueting Suite at Lord's and started at 4.30 pm. The new President, Colin Ingleby-Mackenzie, took the chair and introduced Brian Thornton. Having explained the need, the proposed solution, and the plan for implementation, and given the cost as £3.5 million, he offered members the opportunity to ask questions.

Cost had always been likely to prove the major problem, and the members were well aware of the difficulties. David Hudd, Chairman of Finance, pressed Thornton to confirm that the cost would not exceed £3.5 million and, perhaps unwisely, Thornton did so. The members then gave their approval to proceed by an eighty-three per cent majority.

The installation of the piles to support the Media Centre started on 13 January 1997, but it soon became clear that the budget figure for even the construction of the pylons was inade-

Left: Construction of the concrete pylons ran late. Much work still needed to be completed at the start of the 1997 cricket season.

Right: The 'roof' or top half of the pod, pre-assembled at Falmouth to ensure the sections fitted together accurately.

quate. The quantity surveyor reported that there would be a £230,000 overspend on these Phase 1 works alone. There was even worse news when the tenders for the pod came in. The lowest, from Pendennis, indicated that the budget would be overspent by some £1.2 million.

The project was now in deep trouble. There was a deadline for completion, since the media had to be properly accommodated for the World Cup. Pendennis needed to be given an order by no later than April 1997, or the firm would miss the completion date. The company also said that it would be unable to hold its price if the order was late, because the cost of aluminium was rising fast.

Between January and April 1997 the design team made strenuous efforts to effect savings. The Working Party, which had been strengthened by the presence of Robert Griffiths, QC, and Maurice de Rohan, a structural engineer, looked at the possibility of switching from the Future Systems design and going back to

the David Morley's solution. In the end it was decided that it was now too late for such a drastic step.

With the pressure on him mounting by the day, Thornton asked Maurice de Rohan if he would take over as Chairman of the Working Party. De Rohan reluctantly agreed, allowing Thornton to concentrate his efforts on the timely completion of the new Grand Stand.

Construction of the two pylons which support the pod ran late, and some work was still needed at the start of the cricket season. However, the main activity during the summer of 1997 was the fabrication and assembly of the aluminium sections forming the pod, which was carried out partly at Pendennis's yard in Falmouth. Because the yard was heavily committed to the construction of some super-yachts, a significant amount of the work had to be done at a yard in Holland.

The pod was formed by piecing together thirty-two sections;

Left: Assembly of the pod in progress.

Right: One of the aluminium sections being lowered into position before being welded to its neighbour.

sixteen for the bottom half and sixteen, replicating them, above. All had to be fabricated with precision accuracy so that, when they were brought to site, they would fit together exactly. The design required the sections to be butt-welded together along the edges of the external aluminium plate. Each section was 20 metres long by 3.6 metres wide and weighed up to 6 tonnes. They were first assembled in the yard at Falmouth to ensure that a good fit could be achieved, and then transported to Lord's on lorries escorted by the police.

The precision fabrication of the aluminium, the assembly on site, the erection and eventual welding of the sections all amounted to a very demanding engineering project. When the shell was in place the glass wall had to fit exactly into the space provided – and it did. Great credit must go to David Glover of Ove Arup and Henk Wiekens and his team at Pendennis. The assembly took much longer than originally planned, which was

an embarrassment for the MCC, more particularly because work had to proceed throughout the 1998 cricket season. However, the very high standard of the workmanship went some way to mitigate this predicament.

The pod was assembled and welded together above the supporting pylons, and was lowered into position in May 1998. The fitting out of the interior took a further nine months. Access to the inside is obtained from two lifts, one inside each pylon. On arrival, the lift doors open into a blue, naturally-lit space, which accommodates the bar and restaurant. The blue colour, which pervades the whole internal space, was chosen so that, when seen from outside through the glass wall, its appearance would be neutral and would not distract players.

There is a distinctly nautical feel to the whole inside, which is enhanced by the very high standard of finish usually associated with yacht building. Two hundred journalists can be accommo-

dated, immediately behind the glass wall, at desks on a raked platform that provides perfect sight lines to the playing area. The desks occupy most of the 42-metre span of the building and are served by 26 kilometres of computer and television cable and 500 outlets for telephones and computers.

Above the journalists' desks eleven radio and television commentary boxes are located on a mezzanine floor. Considerable care has been taken to look after the comfort of the correspondents, who have fresh-air nozzles (as in an aeroplane) built into their desks. The building faces the afternoon sun, so it was necessary to fit blinds to minimise the glare.

Sir David Rowland, Chairman of NatWest Group, opened the completed building on 27 April 1998. This revolutionary centre was received with acclamation by the media, the architectural profession and, most importantly, by the members of MCC. It won no fewer than eight architectural awards, including the RIBA's most prestigious Stirling Prize for Architecture. Unfortunately there had been two casualties along the way. Peter Bell stepped down from the Working Party when he found he was in disagreement with Brian Thornton over the latter's management of the architects, and Thornton resigned as Chairman of the Estates Sub-Committee, taking responsibility upon himself for the very large difference between the original budget of £3.5 million and the actual cost of £5.8 million. In his resignation speech Thornton said:

> I confess that the honour of holding this position during a period of such great activity has been one of the most onerous but enjoyable responsibilities that I have ever carried. Despite the cost problems of the Media Centre, I believe the new buildings which have been commissioned during my steward-

Top: Journalists' desks with the air nozzles clearly visible.

Bottom: Journalists at their desks during the 1998 World Cup.

ship will stand the Club in good stead and will preserve Lord's as the headquarters of cricket world-wide and as the only ground where every cricketer wants to play.

In conclusion, he quoted Sir Christopher Wren's words, *Si monumentum requiris, circumspice* – 'If you want my monument, look around you.'

Comments by the architectural correspondents of the press were highly favourable. In the *Daily Telegraph* of 14 May 1999, Giles Worsley wrote:

> The new NatWest Media Centre at Lord's, which springs to life today with the start of the World Cup, is as perfect an expression of the naked reality of power as the glossy skyscrapers of Wall Street soaring above New York. Sport used to be an intimate affair, in which what mattered was the relationship between the crowds in the ground and the players on the field. No longer. Today those spectators are mere colour, atmospherics for the real audience – the millions in their sitting rooms or cheering in pubs. Television is king, and the huge, all-seeing eye of the Media Centre is its physical manifestation.

Rowan Moore in the *Evening Standard* of 27 April 1999 wrote: 'It is a tour de force on the part of the architects, the boat builders and its engineers . . . The point of it is, it raises the spirits.' Similar enthusiasm came from Derek Pringle in the *Independent* on 28 April 1999: 'A triumph of both form and function, it offers up to 200 journalists a stunning vantage point,' while Nonie Niesewand in the same paper on 11 June called it 'One of this century's best buildings in Britain.'

Plaudits continued to roll in throughout the year. Marcus

One of two sweeping spiral staircases leading to the row of commentary boxes. The building's maritime feel is perhaps a reflection of where it was fabricated.

Binney in *The Times* on 5 November wrote: 'It's goodbye to anonymous slab architecture. Britain's building of the year award, the £20,000 Stirling Prize will go to a building of star quality. Topping the list for sheer inventiveness is the new press box at Lord's.' Finally, *Smart Buildings* decided: 'The Client must be applauded for its remarkable vision and broadmindedness. It is organic in form, prefabricated, recyclable, high-tech and last but not least, visually spectacular.'

The building won the following awards:

- Aluminium Imagination Architectural Award – Main Prize
- 1999 British Institute of Architectural technology – Main Commendation
- 1999 British Construction Industry – Building Award
- 1999 RIBA The Stirling Prize for Architecture – RIBA Building of the Year
- RIBA Category Awards Architecture in Arts and Leisure Award
- Institute of Structural Engineers – Structural Achievement Award
- ICE London Merit Award 2000.

For all its merits, the Media Centre is not without its critics. Sir Colin Stansfield-Smith – a past Chairman of the Estates Committee, and now Professor of Architecture at Portsmouth University – had some sharp remarks to make about it. The building, in his view, 'demonstrates an interesting contradiction':

To win the Stirling Prize at a time when 'sustainability' was the big issue for the architectural profession, was not just a surprise but a challenge to credibility. This in some ways indicates the power of its iconic presence.

This is a building designed for use eighteen days a year; it is, however, air-conditioned for the whole year. It is located on the edge of a green field in central London where natural ventilation could, perhaps should, have been possible. As a sealed box, it is disconnected from its own audience, and the only way the journalists know how the crowd are reacting is through their own electronic media.

Contradiction has been an inherent part of architecture in the late twentieth century, and perhaps that is why this building becomes all the more intriguing.

The Media Centre has become an icon of Lord's, instantly recognisable anywhere in the world.

22

Relaying the Outfield

2001–03

The idea of reconstructing the outfield had its roots in the five-year plan launched in 1999, when each committee was asked to consolidate its aspirations for the period 2000 to 2004. One of the principal objectives of the Cricket Committee was 'to play more cricket at Lord's'.

Tony Dodemaide, who had recently arrived as the new MCC Head of Cricket, interpreted this objective in two ways. Besides the obvious solution – to look for opportunities of increasing the number of match days in the schedule – there was a second, less obvious possibility: to enable more play on the days when matches were already scheduled.

Dodemaide had already observed deficiencies in what is arguably the most important component of the ground – the playing arena. Millions had been spent on the surrounding accommodation for spectators and the media, but, apart from routine maintenance, the field itself had remained virtually untouched since 1874, when MCC had last renovated the playing area.

Under the famous slope, which falls almost nine feet from the Grand Stand to the Tavern side, the soil was predominantly heavy London clay, softened by a thick layer of thatch turf, which gave a

Subsoil was removed and taken to landscaping fill in Regent's Park and other sites outside London.

Top: Sand is spread around the oasis of the square.

Centre top: The Pavilion looks out over a desert of sand.

Bottom two pictures: Heavy machinery lifting and removing the clay subsoil from the ground.

spongy feeling under foot. Although a good-quality PVC drainage system had been installed in the mid-1990s, surface water could only reach the pipes sparingly, and certainly not fast enough to facilitate quick recovery after heavy rain. Once the clay had become saturated, water would lie on or near the surface for hours, leading to lengthy delays in play. Around major match periods a cumbersome and labour-intensive method of rolling out numerous plastic sheets had been employed, often in vain attempts to protect a proportion of the surface.

Even worse was the fact that, frequently, little standing water was visible, even though the ground was saturated. The thick layer of thatch meant that, although spectators could see no obvious reason for delay, the umpires and players would feel the water squelching round their boots.

To investigate ways of tackling the problem, Dodemaide and Mick Hunt, the Head Groundsman, visited several cricket grounds in Australia and New Zealand during October and November 2000. The selected grounds had used various methods to improve the resilience of their playing surfaces, and some had tried other techniques to improve the overall flexibility of their fields. Among these innovations was the use of portable pitches – playing surfaces nurtured and prepared in metal trays away from the arena, and therefore a more controlled environment, which can be fitted into the centre square in advance of match days. The Sydney Cricket Ground, for instance, was undergoing a full reconstruction at the time (including replacement of the centre square table), and the Melbourne Cricket Ground, which had undergone a similar reconstruction several years before, was then installing a number of portable pitches for the forthcoming season.

Back in England, Dodemaide sought opinions on ways of improving the drainage at Lord's from local professional bodies, including the Sports Turf Research Institute (STRI) and Grass Science. A range of alternatives was suggested, from a gradual process of heavy top-dressings with sand to the belt-and-braces method of a full reconstruction, which would cost around £1 million.

After a full discussion at a meeting on 14 March 2001, the Cricket Committee decided that action must be taken, and that a full reconstruction was the best bet. Not only would the most expensive option give maximum control over the condition of the surface: it would also provide the resilience and load-bearing ability to accommodate further possible innovations, such as the use of portable pitches, if this proved workable in English conditions.

A working group was set up to take the matter forward. The members were Dodemaide, the Deputy Chief Executive David Batts, the Cricket Committee Chairman Ted Dexter and the Estates Committee Chairman Maurice de Rohan. Their brief was to consider all options and risks, and to prepare a proposal for the Executive Board and Committee.

The sports turf industry was well acquainted with the type of reconstruction being considered, but no cricket ground in the northern hemisphere had undertaken such a major project. Even smaller reconstructions, such as those commonly carried out at football league grounds, create several problems – and the Lord's project was much larger, since the playing area is about two-and-a-half times the size of a soccer pitch. The centre square would have to remain untouched, with the reconstructed ground carefully matching it at the interface, especially around the bowlers' run-ups.

Most importantly, this kind of work would normally be undertaken in the summer, to make the most of better weather, and also to allow the new turf to establish itself steadily from seed. To dig up Lord's in the summer would mean closing the ground for much of the season, and cancelling some of the major matches for which the ground was already contracted.

Of course, this was considered impractical, and a compromise was reached, whereby the Lord's season would finish shortly after the last major game (the C&G Final) at the end of August. The contractor would then have the best chance of getting reasonable weather in the early stages of the project, when some 16,000 tonnes of soil and turf would have to be dug out and removed from the site. Wet weather would make this task considerably more difficult. The ground also had to be ready for play at the beginning of the next season, with a standard of outfield at or near its former level.

Since it was very unlikely that normal seed would germinate and thicken fast enough in the cold of winter and early spring, the only alternative was for turf to be grown in advance, off-site, and transplanted to Lord's once the sub-surface work had been completed. This meant that a turfing sub-contractor had to be engaged in advance of the main project, to sow and nurture a field of specified grass blend – a task that would have to be started early in the spring if the turf was to be mature enough for transplanting at the right time, probably towards the end of December.

Another issue to consider was the type of stabilising system to be employed to help bind the turf roots and sandy sub-soil, and give the surface the best possible load-bearing capability. Several options were available, including the Motz, Deso, Fibreturf and Strathayr mesh systems. In these early stages the Club engaged the assistance of Dr John Lill, a former Secretary of the Melbourne Cricket Club, who had overseen similar works at his own ground and proved a valuable guiding hand in setting the initial parameters of the project.

Having received a briefing on 20 November 2001, the MCC

Top: The first of the hallowed turf is removed from the outfield in September 2002. Many turf rolls were sold and the £35,000 proceeds passed to the MCC foundation.

Centre top: The ground as it appeared after a heavy rain on the base root-zone of sand.

Centre bottom: New turf is laid at last.

Bottom: Turf gradually covering the sandy desert.

Executive Board agreed to recommend to the MCC Committee that the project should proceed in 2002, subject to a satisfactory budget and risk-assessment. This was ratified by Committee on 12 December 2001, and a budget provision of £1 million was included in the 2002 business plan.

Early in 2002 STRI were appointed project managers, and set about determining details with Dodemaide, the internal project director. After much thorough investigation, it was decided to use a Fibreturf stabilising element, a volume of fine, hair-like filaments mixed into the upper root-zone that helps bind the grass roots to the sandy mix and provide load-bearing support in the upper profile. After consultation with the Head Groundsman, STRI specified a seed blend of 30% perennial rye grass, 25% smooth-stalked meadow grass, 20% chewings fescue, 20% per cent slender creeping red fescue and 5% browntop bent variety, which would produce the desired characteristics of resilience, resistance to disease and good appearance.

The specification of layers beneath the surface was equally detailed. Above the geotextile and new drainage trenches at the lowest level, four layers of new material would form the profile necessary to achieve the desired infiltration rate, but at the same time retain enough moisture to ensure that the grass could remain healthy and provide firmness and stability for players. The bottom layer, of coarse aggregate for drainage, was covered by a binding layer of finer material, and the base root-zone of finer sands was spread above. Finally, the upper root-zone, just below the surface, contained still finer sands, as well as around twenty per cent organic material and the reinforcing elements.

Another essential ingredient was a state-of-the-art, computerised irrigation system. Besides distributing regular and exact amounts of water to maintain the right moisture content of the outfield via a matrix of around seventy sprinkler heads set just below the playing surface, the system would enable the groundsmen to irrigate at any time, and not just during working hours, when evaporation rates would be highest.

These detailed plans were included in the comprehensive tender documents prepared by STRI, as were various local stipulations and restrictions on traffic movements to and from the site. MCC had to consider the impact on people living near the ground, as 1,600 heavy truck movements would be required during the project.

With the specification for turf and root-zone decided, the sub-contract for growing 1.8 hectares of turf was put out to tender, and won by Inturf, based at Grantham, in Lincolnshire, where a field was sown in late February and early March 2002. The tender for the main project was put out in May, and after careful assessments and interviews was awarded to John Mallinson Ltd. The Executive Board and Committee were then advised that the overall cost would be £1.26 million, including contingency – and with confirmation that the turf was growing well in Lincolnshire, the Club was committed to a start in the autumn.

On Sunday, 1 September, MCC launched a brief marketing exercise, whereby turf stripped from the old surface was sold in squares or small rolls to interested members and others. Beside the fun and publicity generated, the exercise raised around £35,000, which was passed to the MCC Foundation to benefit junior cricket causes.

By the end of that week the main operation was in full swing, with heavy machinery removing the entire outfield to a depth of about eighteen inches. This rather violent and destructive process certainly provided some anxious moments for members, who were used to regarding the field as sacred and untouchable. Nevertheless, with time of the essence, the subsoil and remaining turf were quickly removed and taken to various destinations, from landscape-fill in Regent's Park to general waste-fill sites around the M25. During this period, the workmen and staff were intrigued to find various earthenware fragments and oyster shells among the rubble, and a selection is now displayed in the Lord's Museum. Fortunately the weather gods were kind, and predominantly dry conditions allowed good progress. Relatively few problems were encountered, and those that did crop up were generally resolved quickly – a testament to the detailed research conducted by the project managers and the good working relationship established within the project team. In fact, of the £50,000 contingency originally budgeted, only £6,000 was eventually required.

The field, carefully laser-graded to pre-set levels with sophisticated and computerised heavy earth-moving equipment, was ready to receive the transplanted turf on schedule, in mid-December. Assuming that the pre-grown turf could be harvested evenly and with similar care, the finished ground would have the best possible chance of displaying evenness and excellent ball-roll characteristics, come the first game of the season. Although laying was effectively finished early in the New Year, the contractor retained responsibility for the initial settling until 14 March 2003. By then the surface had achieved an even consistency, and it reached a generally good standard by the time of the first county match on 23 April.

The project finished on time and below budget – a very satisfactory result, considering the unknowns and risks involved. The underground profile responded well and quickly to some testing rains in the early part of the new season, and it should continue to improve, and perform to the drainage standards originally envisaged as the turf matures.

Finale

by Matthew Fleming, Former Captain of Kent and England One-Day All Rounder

The secret of Lord's is that it is cricket. Trent Bridge, the Oval, Edgbaston – they are all fine grounds. But if you close your eyes anywhere in any of those arenas, they smell, sound and taste like cricket grounds.

Lord's smells, sounds and tastes like cricket. Wherever you are – in the dressing rooms, the Long Room, stepping out on to the hallowed turf or playing on it – your senses reel. You are part of history.

The very idea of Lord's sends shivers up my spine. I have sat in both dressing-rooms as a player for Eton and Kent, and as a squad member for England. The great names on the honours boards humble and inspire – and that, I think, is the secret of Lord's: it humbles and inspires.

Right from its arrival in St John's Wood in 1814, MCC has always done its best to create and maintain a special place in which to play and watch the game. The text and illustrations of this book add up to a stirring record of how Lord's has evolved into a showpiece of modern British architecture.

It is a tremendous tribute to all the people who have improved the ground over the years that they have preserved the spirit of the place. If they had made any bad mistakes, the magic spell would have been broken. The miracle is that it remains intact.

Sources

Baker, Herbert, *Cecil Rhodes by His Architect*. Oxford University Press, 1934.

Baker, Herbert, *Architecture and Personalities*. Country Life, London, 1944.

Birley, Derek, *A Social History of English Cricket*. Aurum Press, London, 1999.

Green, Benny (Editor), *The Lord's Companion*. Pavilion Books, London, 1987.

Harris, Lord, and Ashley Cooper, F. S., *Lord's and the MCC*. London & Counties Press Association, 1914.

Irving, Robert Grant, *Indian Summer*. Yale University Press, London, 1981.

Lewis, A. R., *Double Century*. Hodder & Stoughton, London, 1987.

Rait Kerr, Diana, & Peebles, Ian, *Lord's 1946–1970*. Harrap, London, 1971.

Ridley, Jane, *The Architect and His Wife*. Chatto & Windus, London, 2002.

Slatter, W. H., *Recollections of Lord's and the MCC*. Privately printed, 1914.

Swanton, E. W. (Editor), *Barclays World of Cricket*. Guild Publishing, Glasgow, 1986.

Taylor, A. D., *Annals of Lord's and History of the MCC*. Arrowsmith, 1903.

Warner, Sir Pelham, *Lord's 1787–1945*. Harrap, London, 1946.

Wisden Cricketers' Almanack 1864–1901.

James Lillywhite's Cricketers' Annual 1872–1901.

Unpublished

Marylebone Cricket Club Minutes 1835–2004.